Authentic Reading

Authentic Reading

A course in reading skills for upper-intermediate students

Catherine Walter

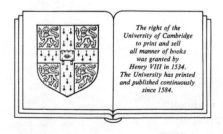

The right of the
University of Cambridge
to print and sell
all manner of books
was granted by
Henry VIII in 1534.
The University has printed
and published continuously
since 1584.

Cambridge University Press
Cambridge
New York   Port Chester
Melbourne   Sydney

To my mother

Published by the Press Syndicate of the University of Cambridge
The Pitt Building, Trumpington Street, Cambridge CB2 1RP
40 West 20th Street, New York, NY 10011, USA
10 Stamford Road, Oakleigh, Melbourne 3166, Australia

© Cambridge University Press 1982

First published 1982
Fifth printing 1991

Book design by Peter Ducker MSTD

Printed in Hong Kong by
Wing King Tong Company Limited

ISBN 0 521 28359 0 Student's Book
ISBN 0 521 28360 4 Teacher's Book

KY

Contents

Part 1   *Instructions: How to do things*

Part 2   *Descriptions: What things are like*

Part 3 Processes: How things happen

Part 4 Narrative: What happened

Part 5 Persuasion: Why you should do it

Part 6   Categories: How things are classified

Acknowledgements

I should like to thank the following people, whose advice and suggestions have been most helpful: Janice Abbott, Henry Daniels, Viviane Dunn, Sue Girolami and Helen Walter. Special thanks to Michael Swan for his many useful comments, and my gratitude to Janet Parrott, Catherine Pigeon and Celia Russo for their support.

The author and publishers are grateful to the authors, publishers and others who have given permission for the use of copyright material identified in the text. It has not been possible to identify the sources of all the material used and in such cases the publishers would welcome information from copyright owners.
The Central Office of Information for the extract on p. 14, © The Crown; Mrs H. Thurber for the cartoon by James Thurber on p. 25, © 1963 by James Thurber; Southwestern Bell Telephone Company for the advertisement on p. 26; *Time* Inc. for the adapted article on p. 28, © *Time* Inc. 1979; Punch Publications Ltd for the two cartoons on pp. 30 and 75; Maurice Temple Smith Ltd for the extracts from *Loneliness* on pp. 32 and 34, © 1973; Trusthouse Forte Hotels for the advertisement on p. 37; The Bodley Head (U.K.) and William Morrow and Co. (U.S.) for the extract on pp. 38–40, © 1974 by Robert M. Pirsig; Her Majesty's Stationery Office for the extract on p. 42, © H.M.S.O.; Phyllis Rosser for the extract on pp. 48–9; the *Guardian* for the adapted article on pp. 52–3; Penguin Books Ltd for the extracts on pp. 46 and 82–3, © Penguin Books 1976; Curtis Brown Ltd for the extract on p. 56, © Doris Lessing 1972; Barnaby's Picture Library for the photographs on pp. 57 and 82; Ms Margaret Seekree for the letter on p. 60; Hugh Vickers for the extracts on pp. 64–5, © Hugh Vickers 1979; Michael ffolkes for the cartoons on pp. 64 and 91, © Michael ffolkes 1979; *The Observer* for the extract on pp. 68–9; V.A.G. (United Kingdom) Ltd for the advertisement on p. 73; the Save the Children Federation for the advertisement on p. 78; *The Financial Times* for the article on p. 86; Rosabeth Kanter for the extract on p. 88; Lenore Kandel for the poem on p. 92 from *I took my mind a walk* ed. George Sanders (Penguin Books).
The photograph on page 53 was taken by Nigel Luckhurst; the drawings on page 66 are by Leslie Marshall.

To the student

Acknowledgements

Careful studies have been done on people who read their own language well. The studies show that almost all of these people get information from a difficult text in the same way:

1 First they read the text once, slowly, with pauses to think about what they have read.
2 Then they read the text at least once more, pausing from time to time to look at other parts of the text. This is in order to see the connections between different parts of the text, and to build a summary in their minds.

A very large percentage of people who read in this way remember both general ideas and details better than people who read in other ways.

Of course, if you are not used to reading English in this way, deciding to change is not enough. So each text in *Authentic Reading* has a *Summary skills* or similar exercise first. This exercise does not ask you to *write* a summary, but it demands that you look back at the text and organize the information in it. By the time you have finished the book, you will have had enough practice to do this yourself with any text you read.

In addition to summary building, there are other reading skills which are particularly important when you read a foreign language. Certain skills will be necessary for every text you read in English: guessing unknown words, for example. Others, like understanding complicated sentences, will only be needed for certain types of text. In this book, you will practise these skills with specially designed exercises. Each set of exercises is based on the particular problems of the text it follows.

All of the texts in this book are real samples of written English. You will find newspaper articles, advertisements, passages from novels, part of an instruction booklet, letters and poetry. None of them were written especially for foreigners. This means that some texts may be easier to understand than others; but even the easier texts will help you to read better. The exercises accompanying difficult texts will give you ways of dealing with other texts outside the classroom. Remember that you can get a lot of information from a text without understanding every word.

I have given definitions for a few words in some texts. These words are important to an understanding of the text, and are difficult or impossible to guess. Some difficult words are not defined, but these are not important to an understanding of the text: do not worry about them. Remember, too, that the definitions given are for the words as they are used in the text; you may want to check with your teacher or look in a good dictionary before using the same word in another situation.

There are no multiple-choice questions in *Authentic Reading*. There are several reasons for this. One is that while people who have good summary skills do well on multiple-choice tests, the reverse is not always true. So if you are preparing for an examination that includes this type of question, *Authentic Reading* will help you.

This book was written for use in the classroom. However, if you want to use it on your own, there is a key to the exercises in the Teacher's Book.

To the teacher

Authentic Reading offers upper intermediate students a selection of authentic texts and a series of exercises specially designed to improve their reading skills.

The texts

There are 24 texts, all of them taken from authentic British and American sources. (Each American text is indicated as such in its introduction.) Three of the texts have been adapted slightly; the changes are of the sort a native speaker would expect in an abridged novel. The remaining 21 texts are printed just as they appear in the original. I have chosen texts that might be read by an adult of average intelligence and varied interests. A few are literary, and others are taken from newspapers, magazines and brochures.

The authenticity of the texts means, of course, that length and difficulty vary slightly. The exercises accompanying the more difficult texts are designed to provide students with strategies for approaching new texts outside the classroom. The four texts forming each part were all written for the same sort of reason (sometimes called function); for example, persuasion or description. Within this framework the four texts are very different from one another. You may want to stop and glance through a part now to get an idea of the variety.

A note on glosses: I have only glossed a word if its meaning is vital to the comprehension of the text, and if it cannot be guessed from the context. The glosses are not dictionary definitions: any gloss should be taken to cover only the way the word is used in the text.

The exercises

As I have explained in the note 'To the student', the first exercise to accompany each text is a *Summary Skills* exercise. In some cases this exercise comes before the text and directs the students to search for specific information within it. Doing this sort of exercise systematically will help students to develop efficient reading strategies. For a detailed discussion of the rationale behind this approach, see the Introduction to the Teacher's Book.

In addition to the *Summary Skills* work, each unit contains a range of other exercises. There are some 15 types of exercise in all; each unit contains types designed to help with the particular problems posed by the text at hand. By working their way through the units, students will learn to avoid the most common causes of misunderstanding written English. The Teacher's Book gives suggestions as to the classroom exploitation of all the exercises, as well as a key to the answers.

Additional activities

Many teachers will wish to use the texts in the Student's Book as springboards for other classroom and homework activities, such as discussion, writing practice, etc. Detailed suggestions for work of this kind are given in the 'Additional Activities' sections of the Teacher's Book. These include for each unit:

1 Complete instructions for a classroom activity practising speaking skills, and approaching the theme of the text from a different standpoint. This might be a task-based discussion, a role play activity, a class survey, etc.
2 Suggestions for more intensive vocabulary work, designed to help students incorporate some of the words from the text into their active usage.
3 An idea for a guided writing exercise based on the theme of the unit.

Part 1   Instructions: How to do things

Unit 1   Danger from fire

This is part of a booklet distributed by local fire brigades in Great Britain.

Read the text *slowly*. Pause as often as you like. It will be easier to answer the questions if you imagine you have to make a summary of the text.

Read the text *twice*. The second time, take as much time as you need, and try to see how the different parts of the text fit together.

Then do the exercises. Do not worry if you cannot answer all the questions without referring to the text. This is normal: The exercises are to teach you, not test you.

In the bedroom

1.   Don't smoke in bed — it causes about 1,000 fires a year, many with fatal results.
2.   Don't overload your electrical points: the ideal is 'one appliance, one socket'.
3.   Don't use an electric underblanket over you or an overblanket under you. An underblanket, unless of the low-voltage type, MUST be switched off before you get into bed.
4.   Never let furnishings or clothing get close to a lighted fire. Make sure that there is a suitable guard for the room heater.
5.   Keep aerosol-type containers away from heat and NEVER burn or puncture them.
6.   Don't dim a table lamp by covering it: buy a low-wattage bulb.
7.   Pyjamas and nightdresses, especially for children and elderly people, should be made from flame-resistant material.

If cut off by fire

8.   Close the door of the room and any fanlight or other opening and block up any cracks with bedding etc.
9.   Go to the window and try to attract attention.
10.   If the room fills with smoke, lean out of the window unless prevented by smoke and flame coming from a room below or nearby. If you cannot lean out of the window, lie close to the floor where the air is clearer until you hear the fire brigade.
11.   If you have to escape before the fire brigade arrives, make a rope by knotting together sheets or similar materials and tie it to a bed or other heavy piece of furniture.
12.   If you cannot make a rope and the situation becomes intolerable, drop cushions or bedding from the window to break your fall, get through the window feet first, lower yourself to the full extent of your arms and drop.
13.   If possible drop from a position above soft earth. If above the first floor, drop only as a last resort.

(Prepared for the Home Office and the Scottish Home and Health Department by the Central Office of Information 1975.)

fanlight: a window over a door.
appliance: something that uses electricity in the home (heater, washing machine, etc.)
aerosol-type containers: these have gas in them to help spray out liquid or foam.

Summary skills 1

Here is a picture of a dangerous bedroom. Each of the lines shows one of the
dangers in the numbered instructions. Match the lines with their numbers.

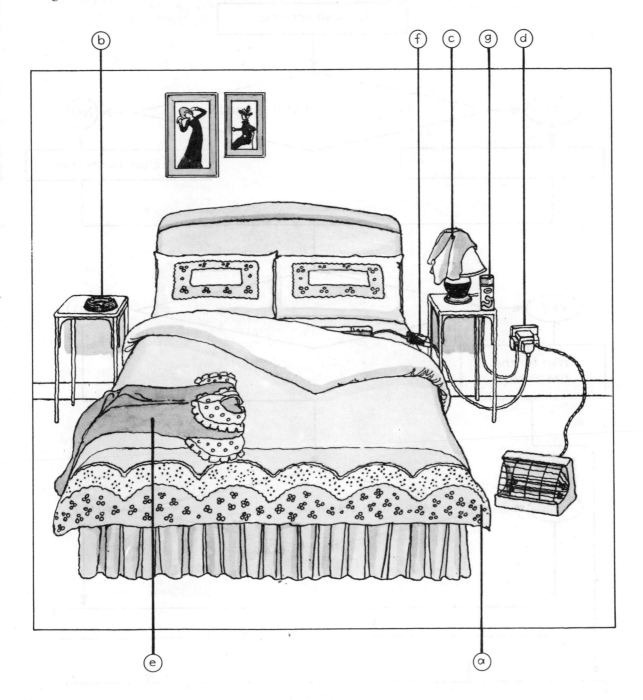

Summary skills 2

Complete this chart with information from 'If cut off by fire'.

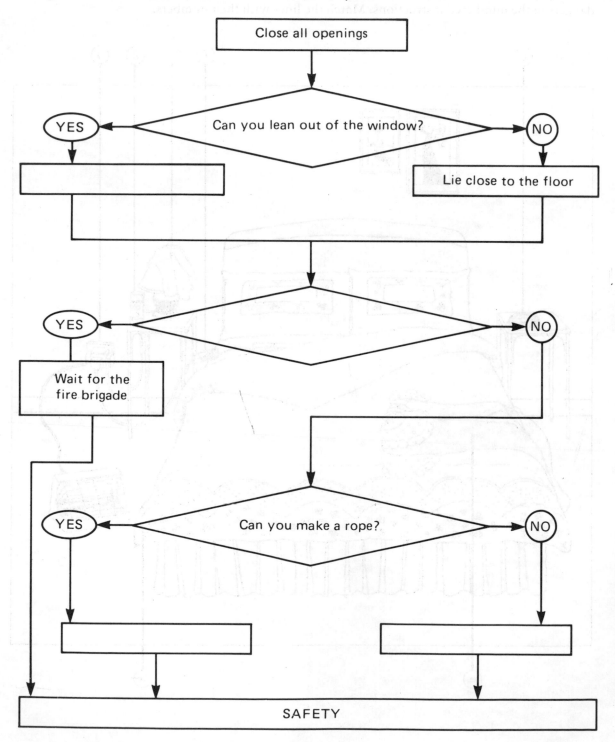

Guessing unknown words

Three things can help you guess words you don't know:
– what you find in the text,
– what you know about similar words, and
– what you know about the world.
Guess the probable meaning of each word. More help is given with the first three words.

1 *socket* (point 2): 'Don't overload' and 'one appliance' show you that an electrical point and a socket are probably the same thing. And if you use a socket with an appliance, it is probably the place where you put a
   ....

2 *dim* (point 6): If you can dim a lamp by covering it, then *dim* probably means
   ....

3 *elderly* (point 7): Part of this word looks like another word you know. If these people need special care in the home, like children, *elderly* probably means ....

4 *break your fall* (point 12) probably means make your fall ....

5 *to the full extent of your arms* (point 12) probably means with your arms
   ....

6 *only as a last resort* (point 13) probably means only if you ....

Accurate comprehension

You may want to look back at the text while answering these questions. Write **T** if the sentence is true according to the text, **F** if the sentence is false according to the text, and **DS** if the text doesn't say.

1 Smoking in bed causes about 1,000 fatal fires a year.
2 You should not go to sleep with an electric overblanket over you.
3 You should keep clothes away from a lighted fire.
4 If you cover a bulb, you must make sure it is a low-wattage one.
5 Children and old people are often burnt to death because their pyjamas or nightdresses catch fire.
6 If you are cut off by fire, you should try to stop smoke coming into the room.
7 If smoke and flames are coming from a room below, it is best to go to the window and shout for help.
8 You can escape by tying sheets to a heavy piece of furniture and throwing it out of the window.
9 If you jump out of a window, you should try to make your landing as soft as possible.

Unit 2   Wear and care of soft contact lenses

Read these instructions for contact lens wearers. Read them as slowly as you wish. You may want to do the *Summary skills* exercises while you are reading, or you may prefer to do them afterwards. In any case, you will want to check your answers with the text.

Preparation

As with all contact lenses, cleanliness is of paramount importance. If these simple rules are followed, you will find using soft contact lenses to be simple and convenient.

a. Always wash and rinse your hands thoroughly before handling your lenses. Shake off excess water and handle your lenses with damp hands. If you find this difficult dry your hands ensuring that no lint or paper remains on the skin.

b. Ensure your nails are clean and preferably short before handling your lenses. Your lenses may be damaged if they are handled with your finger nails.

c. Do not use oily lotions before handling your lenses. Apply make-up after your lenses are in position.

Lens Profile

Before insertion, it is important to check that the lens is not inside out. This is easily done. Place your lens on your index finger and look at the outline shape of the lens as in the illustration below. If the edge is a continuous curve it is correct. If the edge turns out slightly it is inside out and should be reversed, then rinsed with saline. All lenses have individual markings. If these can be read on the convex side the lens is correct, if however the figures are on the concave side, the lens is inside out as the marking is always placed on the outside of the lens.

Lens Insertion

After thoroughly washing and rinsing your hands, follow these steps to insert the lens:

1. Place the lens on the tip of the index finger of your dominant hand.

2. Pull up the upper eyelid with your other hand.

3. Pull the lower lid down using the middle finger of your dominant hand.

4. Look upwards, and place the lens on the white of the eye. Gently release the lids. Blink and the lens will centre over the coloured part of the eye. If you need to help centre a lens, close your eyelid and gently massage through the closed lid.

Lens Removal

To remove your lenses, first wash and rinse your hands thoroughly. Have your storage container opened with solution and ready to receive the lenses.

1. Ensure the lens is located over the cornea (the central part of the eye).

2. Look upwards and pull the lower lid down.

3. Using the index finger of your dominant hand, slide the lens onto the white of the eye.

4. Press the lens gently between thumb and index finger, and remove the lens from your eye.

Compressing a moist lens between the thumb and forefinger is not harmful, providing the fingernails do not contact the lens.

(From the instruction booklet published by Hydron Europe.)

dominant hand: the hand you write with.

Summary skills

A   Lens profile

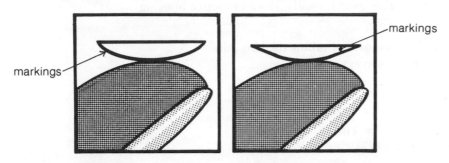

Which of these diagrams shows the correct lens shape? Which is incorrect (inside out)?

B   Lens Insertion

Match the lines with the numbered instructions.

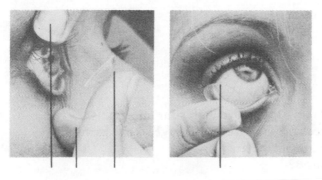

C   Lens Removal

Match the lines with the numbered instructions.

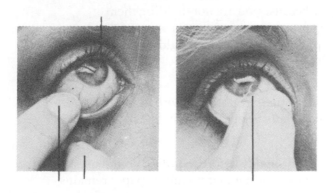

Guessing unknown words

Relationships between words you know and words you don't know can help you understand the new words. This exercise will give you practice in using those relationships.

Example: (lines 34 and 49) lens removal = taking the lens out.
lens insertion = ...

Answer: putting the lens in

1 (line 10)
   drying hands with paper: paper on skin
   drying hands with cloth: lint on skin.
   So *lint* must be ....
2 (lines 27-33)
   marking on convex side = outside = correct
   marking on .... side = inside = incorrect
   So, give names to the sides of this curve:

3 (lines 39-44) The instructions about eyelids say:
   – Pull up the upper eyelid.
   – Then pull the lower lid down.
   – Then gently release the lids.
   So *release* must mean ....
4 (lines 14 and 66)
   'Your lenses may be damaged *if* they are handled with your fingernails.'
   'Compressing a moist lens between the thumb and forefinger is not harmful, *providing* the fingernails do not contact the lens.'
   So, does *providing* mean *if* or *unless*?

Dividing sentences

Some of the sentences in these instructions are complicated. If you have difficulty in understanding, it may be because you are not dividing them correctly. This exercise will help you practise trying different ways of dividing sentences. In each sentence, decide whether the division should come
– just before the part in italics, or
– just after the part in italics.

Example: Shake off excess water / *and handle* your lenses with damp hands.
            (*handle* is a verb here; *and handle* begins the second part of the sentence.)

1 Always wash and rinse your hands *thoroughly* before handling your lenses.
2 If you find this difficult *dry* your hands ensuring that no lint or paper remains on the skin.

3 Ensure your nails are clean *and preferably* short before handling your lenses.
4 If the edge turns out *slightly* it is inside out and should be reversed.
5 ... the lens is inside out *as the marking* is always placed on the outside of the lens.

Inference

What evidence is there in the text for the following?

Example: Soap can damage contact lenses.
Answer: Each part of the instructions begins with directions to wash *and rinse* your hands.

1 Paper can scratch contact lenses.
2 Any oil on a contact lens makes it difficult for the person to see.
3 It is safe to wear most eye make-up with contact lenses.
4 These instructions were written so that both left-handed and right-handed people could follow them.

Unit 3　How to shine at a job interview

This is the first page of an article in an American magazine. Read it carefully, as many times as you like. Then answer the questions.

The smart job-seeker needs to rid herself of several standard myths about interviewing before she starts pounding the pavement looking for a job. What follows is a list of some of these untruths and some tips to help you do your best at your next interview.

Myth 1: The aim of interviewing is to obtain a job offer　　　　　5
Only half true. The real aim of an interview is to obtain the job *you want*. That often means rejecting job offers you don't want! Incompetent job-seekers, however, become so used to accommodating employers' expectations that they often easily qualify for jobs they don't want. So, before you do back-flips for an employer, be sure you want the job.　　　　　10

Myth 2: Always please the interviewer
Not true. Try to please yourself. Giving answers that you think will suit a potential employer, losing touch with your own feelings (in order to get in touch with some other person's feelings) and, in general, practicing an abject policy of appeasement are certain to get you nowhere. Of course, don't be hostile—nobody　15
wants to hire someone disagreeable. But there is plainly a middle ground between being too ingratiating and being hostile. An effective interview (whether you are offered the job or not) is like an exciting encounter in conversation with your seatmate on an airplane.

Myth 3: Try to control the interview　　　　　20
Nobody "controls" an interview—neither you nor the interviewer—although one or both parties often try. Then it becomes a phony exchange between two human beings; no business is likely to be transacted. When somebody tries to control us, we resent it. When we try to control somebody, she resents us. Remember, you can't control what an employer thinks of you, just as she can't　25
control what you think of her. So hang loose when interviewing: Never dominate the interview. Compulsive behavior turns off your authenticity.

Myth 4: Never interrupt the interviewer
No dice. "Never talk when I'm interrupting," said McGeorge Bundy.
Good advice.　　　　　30
Study the style of an effective conversationalist: She interrupts and is interrupted! An exciting conversation always makes us feel free—free to interrupt, to disagree, to agree enthusiastically. We feel comfortable with people who allow us to be natural. So, when interviewing, half the responsibility lies with you. Do you seem uptight? Try being yourself for a change. Employers will either like or dis-　35
like you, but at least you'll have made *an impression*. Leaving an employer indifferent is the worst impression you can make. And the way to make an effective impression is to feel free to be yourself, which frees your interviewer to be *herself!*

Myth 5: Don't disagree with the interviewer　　　　　40
Another silly myth. If you don't disagree at times, you become, in effect, a "yes" woman. Don't be afraid to disagree with your interviewer—in an agreeable way. And don't hesitate to change your mind. The worst that could happen would be that the interviewer says to herself, "There's a person with an open mind!" The conventional wisdom says "be yourself," true enough. But how many people　45
can be themselves if they don't feel free to disagree?

(From an article by Dick Irish in *Glamour*.)

myth: something false, that most people believe is true.　　*out of touch*: out of contact.

Have you got the main ideas?

Here are eight sentences. Only four of them express important ideas from the text. The other ideas are in the text, but they are not the author's main concerns. Choose the four main points. Then compare your answers with some other students before discussing them with your teacher.

1 A good interview is like an exciting meeting during a journey.
2 Remember that you are trying to find a job that satisfies *you*.
3 Change your mind if you want to.
4 Be yourself.
5 Don't try to dominate the conversation with your interviewer.
6 Try to let the interviewer be herself.
7 Don't be aggressive.
8 Don't be overly respectful of your interviewer.

Guessing unknown words

Match each italicized word in column A with its probable meaning in column B. Sometimes you can guess the meaning from the sentence where you find the word; sometimes you will have to look at what comes before and after that sentence. Be careful: there are some extra meanings in column B.

COLUMN A

1 What follows is a list of some of these untruths and some *tips* to help you do your best . . . (line 3)
2 Giving answers that you think will suit a *potential* employer . . . (lines 12–13)
3 . . . *practicing an abject policy of appeasement* . . . (lines 14–15)
4 But there is plainly a *middle ground* between being too ingratiating and being hostile. (line 16)
5 When somebody tries to control us, we *resent* it. (line 24)
6 So *hang loose* when interviewing. (line 26)
7 Study the style of an *effective* conversationalist . . . (line 31)
8 Do you seem *uptight*? (lines 34–35)

COLUMN B

a) relax
b) don't telephone often
c) appreciate
d) nervous
e) possible (in the future)
f) model answers
g) powerful
h) successful
i) doing anything to avoid disagreement
j) suggestions
k) a moderate position
l) dislike, feel as unfair
m) the time between two jobs

How will it continue?

How do you think this article will continue? Here are six sentences: choose the ones that might logically be in the continuation of the article.

1 You can never be too quiet in an interview. Employers value people who can listen.
2 Get the help of the employer who has a job you *don't* want: she might give you information about finding a job you *do* want.
3 A good job-hunter never tells an employer how much she expects to earn: this might make a bad impression.
4 If you are not sure about what kind of job you want, don't waste time interviewing for jobs now! First find people doing jobs you might want to do and make appointments with them to get more information.
5 Don't cancel appointments to interview even after accepting a job offer you do want. Remember, you are never employed until you are on the payroll.
6 If you don't know the answer to a question, don't say 'I don't know'. Give what you think is a probable answer: it may be right.

Unit 4 American telephones

'Well, If I Called the Wrong Number, Why Did You Answer the
Phone?'

Reading for specific information

On the next page is part of *The Telephone Catalog*, a booklet published by an
American telephone company (Southwestern Bell) for its customers. Before you
read the whole text, practise looking for specific information by answering
these questions as quickly as you can.

According to the telephone company, what should you do in the following
situations?
1 You come home one evening and find a telephone bill for $10,000. You are
   sure there is a mistake.
2 You try to phone a friend from the airport: the phone takes your money but
   you can't hear anything at all.
3 You want to build a swimming pool behind your house.
4 From your home, you try to call an American friend in another city. The
   phone is answered by someone speaking a language you don't understand.
5 A visiting child knocks your telephone onto the floor and breaks it.
6 You want to phone a relative who lives 400 miles away, and you are worried
   about spending too much money.
7 Someone you don't know phones and tries to sell you an encyclopedia. You
   say you are not interested but they keep talking.

Other Things You Should Know

Vacation rate. If you're planning to be gone for one month or more, call your service representative to have your phone put on vacation rate. It's lower than most regular rates, but there is a charge to reconnect your service. Also, your calls can be referred to another number while you're away.

Poor connection. If you have a poor connection or are cut off on a Long Distance call, both parties should hang up. If you made the call, tell the Operator and ask to be reconnected; you'll get an adjustment on your next bill.

Damaged or out-of-order telephones. We'll repair or replace them at no extra charge, if they come from Southwestern Bell. (Excepted are Design Line telephone housings beyond the warranty period). Simply call Southwestern Bell Repair Service. The number is listed in the Call Guide (Customer Guide) pages at the front of your directory.

Pay phones out-of-order. If one of our coin phones collects your money but your call doesn't go through, report it by dialing "O" (Operator) from another phone. We'll see that the phone gets fixed and mail you a refund.

PhoneCenter Stores. You can save money by going to the PhoneCenter Store and picking up your telephones. If your home is already equipped with modular jack outlets, you can save even more. For more information, see the PhoneCenter Store section in the front of this Catalog.

Directory Assistance. In some states you may be charged for some calls to Directory Assistance. Please refer to the Call Guide section in your directory for specific charges.

Toll-free numbers. A phone number preceded by 800 is a toll-free number used by many businesses to make it easier for their customers to call them. Remember to dial "1" first.

Wrong numbers. If you reach a wrong number on a Long Distance call, we don't want you to pay. Call the Operator immediately to keep the charge off your bill. If you reach a wrong number from a pay phone, we'll mail you a refund.

Complaint procedures. If you have a complaint about telephone rates and/or service, we encourage you to speak to a service representative in the local business office. If the problem is not resolved, you may ask to speak with the business office supervisor. Our business office is open from 8.30 a.m. to 5 p.m.*, Monday through Friday, for handling inquiries.

Nuisance or obscene calls. If you receive obscene, harrassing or threatening calls, follow these suggestions:

1. Hang up at the first obscene word or if the caller hasn't said anything by the second time you say hello.

2. Give no information, such as your name and address, until the caller has been identified.

3. Advise your children not to give any information to strangers. If you're not home they should say, "Mother/Father can't come to the phone right now."

4. If calls persist, call your business office or the Police.

5. If you don't want to talk to a person selling a product or service by phone, just say, "No thank you", and hang up.

Phone Pick-up/Service Centers. You may have seen Southwestern Bell locations called Phone Pick-up/Service Centers. Unlike PhoneCenter Stores, these are limited service operations where you can pick up a telephone you've already ordered or drop one off for repair. On occasion, you may be directed to a Phone Pick-up/Service Center by your service representative or Repair Service attendant.

Organize your Long Distance calls. Before you make a Long Distance call, make a list of topics you want to cover, then keep an eye on the clock. You'll probably say everything in less time and save money.

Person-to-person. When you're expecting an important person-to-person call but have to leave your home or office, leave word with someone where you can be reached. That way, the Operator will relay the call to you.

Before you dig, call us. Before you excavate on your property, please dial the Operator and ask for Enterprise 9800 (in Metropolitan Houston, call 223-4567). We will tell you if there is any buried telephone cable nearby. One quick call could prevent an interruption of your own telephone service as well as the service over a wide area.

*4.30 p.m. in some areas.

(From an advertisement for the Southwestern Bell Telephone Company.)

Guessing unknown words

Read the entire text, slowly and as many times as you wish. Then find words or groups of words in the text which fit into the blanks in these sentences.
Example (lines 15–22):

You hadn't given me your phone number, so I had to look it up in the

....

Answer: directory (line 22)

1 (lines 15–22) The price of this washing machine includes a one-year .... So we'll repair it free if you have any problems during the first year you own the machine.
2 (lines 23–27) I dialled your number four times but the call didn't .... : I just heard a funny buzzing noise.
3 (lines 23–27) Satisfied or your money back: if you are not perfectly happy with our products, just send them back to us and we will mail you a

....
4 (lines 35–43) You don't have to pay anything to find out more about our company: you can dial our .... from anywhere in the United States.
5 (lines 59–64) When *Lady Chatterly's Lover* was printed in England, some people thought that its description of sexual acts were .... and that the book should not be sold.
6 (lines 76–84) If you're going out shopping, can you .... this coat .... at the cleaners'?
7 (lines 85–94) I'm taking a conversation class in English. During the first lesson the class worked in groups to decide which .... we wanted to discuss during the year.
8 (lines 95–102) The laying of a .... under the Atlantic Ocean to transmit telephone calls between Europe and the United States was a long and difficult job.

Inference

Find evidence in the text for the following statements.
1 The telephone company is trying to reduce the number of vans and cars it uses.
2 The company is trying to discourage people from using Directory Assistance too often.
3 Kidnappers sometimes try to find out by telephone if a child is at home alone.
4 Stocks of telephones are kept at PhoneCenter Stores.

Part 2   Descriptions: What things are like

Unit 5   A city is dying

Read this American news article about the problems of Athens. Read it as slowly as you like, and as many times as you like, before beginning the questions. Look back at it as often as you want while you are doing the exercises: they are meant to help you, not to test your memory.

Stinking buses, their passengers pale and tired, jam the crowded streets. Drivers shout at one another and honk their horns. Smog smarts the eyes
5 and chokes the senses. The scene is Athens at rush hour. The city of Plato and Pericles is in a sorry state of affairs, built without a plan, lacking even adequate sewerage facilities, hemmed in
10 by mountains and the sea, its 135 square miles crammed with 3.7 million people. Even Athens' ruins are in ruin: sulfur dioxide eats away at the marble of the Parthenon and other treasures on the
15 Acropolis. As Greek Premier Constantine Karamanlis has said, 'The only solution for Athens would be to demolish half of it and start all over again.'

So great has been the population flow
20 toward the city that entire hinterland villages stand vacant or nearly so. About 120,000 people from outlying provinces move to Athens every year, with the result that 40% of Greece's citizenry are now
25 packed into the capital. The migrants come for the few available jobs, which are usually no better than the ones they fled. At the current rate of migration, Athens by the year 2000 will have a population of
30 6.5 million, more than half the nation.

Aside from overcrowding and poor public transport, the biggest problems confronting Athenians are noise and pollution. A government study con-
35 cluded that Athens was the noisiest city in the world. Smog is almost at killing levels: 180-300 mg of sulfur dioxide per cubic meter of air, or up to four times the level that the World Health Organization
40 considers safe. Nearly half the pollution comes from cars. Despite high prices for vehicles and fuel ($2.95 per gallon), nearly 100,000 automobiles are sold in Greece each year; 3,000 driver's licenses are issued in Athens monthly.
45

After decades of neglect, Athens is at last getting some attention. In March a committee of representatives from all major public service ministries met to discuss a plan to unclog the city, make it
50 livable and clean up its environment. A save-Athens ministry, which will soon

55 begin functioning, will propose heavy taxes to discourage in-migration, a minimum of $5 billion in public spending for Athens alone, and other projects for the countryside to encourage residents to stay put. A master plan that will move many government offices to the city's fringes is already in the works. 60 Meanwhile, more Greeks keep moving into Athens. With few parks and precious few oxygen-producing plants, the city and its citizens are literally suffocating.

(Adapted from an article in *Time* magazine.)

stinking: smelling very bad, having a very unpleasant odour.
sewerage: a system that moves the human waste from toilets out of the city, to a place where it is treated chemically.
unclog the city: stop it from being so crowded.

Summary skills

Fill in as many of the empty spaces as you can on the table below. Look at the text carefully to do this. Put a question mark if you are not sure of something; it is not necessary to fill all the spaces. When you have finished, compare your answers with those of the people around you.

Problem	Cause(s)	Proposed solution(s)
1 Overcrowding	– Athens' geography	– Moving of government offices
2 Poor public transport	– High rate of migration?	– Demolish ½ of Athens, start again
3 Noise		– Public spending?
4		– Oxygen-producing plants?

Guessing unknown words

Three things can help you guess words you do not know:
– what you find in the text,
– what you know about similar words, and
– what you know about the world.
Guess the probable meaning of each word.

1 *lacking* (line 8): This sentence is describing the problems of Athens; so 'lacking adequate sewerage facilities' probably means .... adequate sewerage facilities.
2 *crammed* (line 11): Because this is a sentence about Athens' problems, 3.7 million people is probably considered a lot of people for 135 square miles. So *crammed* probably means ....
3 *fled* (line 27): The new jobs in Athens are usually no better than the old jobs the migrants ....
4 *confronting* (line 33): 'The problems confronting Athenians' are the problems Athenians ....
5 *decades* (line 46): It is not easy to guess exactly what this word means, but 'at last' tells you that it means ....
6 *stay put* (line 58): This means not to ....
7 *is already in the works* (line 60): This means has already ....

"*Sometimes, Carstairs, I wonder if it's worth it.*"

Facts and figures

Find the information in the text that will help you solve these mathematical problems. Perhaps you will want to work with a friend on some of the problems if you are not used to doing maths.

1 Complete this graph about Athens' growing population.

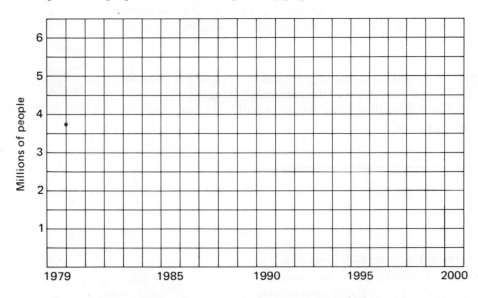

2 How many driver's licences are issued in Athens every year?
3 How many people per square mile were living in Athens when the article was written?
4 What is the present population of Greece?
5 What is the level of sulfur dioxide considered safe by the World Health Organization?

Unit 6 Loneliness

Here are two descriptions from a book about lonely people. Both these women asked to talk to the author when they heard he was interviewing people for the book.

As you read the text, try to make a picture of Mrs Calthorpe and her home in your mind. Then read it again, and add to the picture or change it if you want. Of course, you may read it more than twice if you wish. Then answer the questions on the opposite page.

Mrs Calthorpe

Mrs Calthorpe is forty-three years old. She earns about £10 a week as an office cleaner and receives family income supplement. She is living temporarily in one of the last occupied houses in a clearance area in the centre of a Northern town. Her husband is in   5
prison, not for the first time, for a series of attacks on women, including a rape, and she is left with four children between the ages of eight and sixteen. The street is littered with fragments of broken glass, so that it is virtually impossible to walk without   10
crunching splinters of glass underfoot. Mrs Calthorpe says it's a death-trap for the younger children, who are always coming home with cuts and gashes. Apart from that, vagrants have removed the pieces of zinc from the boarded-up windows, and this allows rats to   15
escape into the street. In the back garden the grass is high and rank; the garden wall has collapsed in several places, so there are heaps of red bricks at intervals. There is a sofa in the middle of the yard, which Mrs Calthorpe says came from the Welfare and proved to   20
be infested.
　　The interior of the house is shabby and fetid. A dog, almost devoid of fur, sleeps under an old coat in the corner. There is a blazing fire, although the day is

warm, and a bag of coal stands beside the grate. Mrs   25
Calthorpe wears no make-up, and looks pale and
drawn. She wears a stained pink sweater and a navy-
blue short skirt. She has no stockings, and her legs are
pale, with the veins standing out, blue and knotted.

---

clearance area: a part of a town that will be destroyed to make room for new buildings or parks.
rape: forcing someone to have sexual intercourse.
vagrants: people without fixed homes or regular jobs.
zinc: a sort of metal.
infested: the sofa has a large number of insects living in it.
shabby and fetid: the house shows signs of wear (for example, torn wallpaper) and smells bad.

How good is your picture of Mrs Calthorpe and her home?

If you have made a fairly good picture in your mind, you will be able to answer
these questions, or find the answers easily by looking back at the text.

Find at least one reason why:
1 The younger children are always coming home with cuts and gashes. (line 13)
2 The sofa is in the middle of the yard. (line 19)
3 The interior of the house is shabby and fetid. (line 22)
4 Mrs Calthorpe looks pale and drawn. (line 26)

Guessing unknown words

Sometimes it is impossible to guess exactly what a word means; but often this is
not necessary in order to understand the text as a whole. For example, *gashes*
(line 13): because of the description of the street, and because of the word *cuts*,
you can guess that a gash is an injury.
   Read the sentences these words are in and guess what the words probably
mean:
1 *littered* (line 9)
2 *crunching* (line 11)
3 *has collapsed* (line 17)
4 *stained* (line 27)

Read this text in the same way as you read the one about Mrs Calthorpe: try to build a picture in your mind. Then do the questions on the opposite page.

Miss Quentin

Miss Quentin is in her late fifties and lives alone in a detached bungalow in a London suburb; the roof is low and the tiles are covered with pale moss and lichen; the front wall is almost entirely covered with ornamental trees. The structure of the bungalow is   5
concealed by plants and trees; everything is reticence, timidity and concealment.

Miss Quentin is a small, attractive woman who is nervous. She wears a long black skirt, silver-threaded slippers, and a wrap that is half-stole, half-shawl, over   10
a modern print blouse. Tea is laid out on hexagonal plates covered with brown and orange designs — sandwiches, bread and butter, cake. In the grate, a gleaming and symmetrical pyramid of half-burnt coals. Low armchairs with floral covers, beams, wooden   15
lamp with parchment frame and low-watt bulb; every-where there are pictures of Miss Quentin's family: smiling, posed, on holiday, relaxed. Miss Quentin is silent at first; the sound of the coals burning with a faint metallic crackle. Miss Quentin had expected to   20
meet an older man; she is not convinced that I will understand.

(From *Loneliness* by Jeremy Seabrook)

a detached bungalow: a low house not attached to other houses.
moss and lichen: small flat plants that spread on stones.
concealed: hidden.
reticence: habit of being silent or uncommunicative.
a wrap that is half-stole, half-shawl: a piece of clothing without sleeves, worn over the shoulders to keep them warm.

Have you got the picture?

Try not to look at the text as you answer these questions. Say as much as you can remember about:
1 The outside of Miss Quentin's house.
2 Miss Quentin's appearance.
3 The inside of Miss Quentin's house.

Accurate comprehension

Read the text again before you do these questions. Then mark each sentence with **T** if it is true according to the text, **F** if it is false according to the text, and **DS** if the text doesn't say.

1 There are a lot of trees around Miss Quentin's house.
2 Miss Quentin is a tidy woman.
3 Miss Quentin wears bright colours like red and orange.
4 The inside of Miss Quentin's house is comfortable-looking.
5 Miss Quentin's family is dead.
6 Miss Quentin is relaxed.

Unit 7   Holidays in Scotland

Reading for specific information

Suggest hotels for the following people by referring to the information on the opposite page. Sometimes more than one hotel may be suitable; in that case, indicate how much each hotel would cost for a seven-night stay.

1   Two women friends who want to do several all-day hikes in the mountains during the spring.
2   A man with two children aged six and ten, who will spend July in Scotland. The ten-year-old would like to play tennis and the father enjoys squash.
3   A handicapped lawyer who must use a wheelchair but drives her own car. She enjoys concerts, museums, fine architecture and swimming. She will spend the first two weeks of October in Scotland.
4   A writer, a teacher and their one-year-old daughter. They want to be in a quiet place during August. They enjoy good food, and like to take long walks (the baby rides in a back-pack).
5   An older couple, aged 65 and 68. They love mountain scenery and still take easy walks in the mountains when they can. They want to see some of Scotland's famous lochs during May.

Guessing unknown words

Here is an exercise to help you guess words you do not know. Match each italicized word in A with the meaning in B that comes closest to it. B has some extra meanings.

A : WORDS
1   (Gatehouse of Fleet) . . . Set in 100 *acres* of private grounds, . . .
2   (Glenborrodale) There can be few better places for a *refreshing* holiday . . .
3   (North Berwick) This fine hotel *overlooks* the famous West Links golf course and the Firth of Forth . . .
4   (North Berwick) . . . has its own open-air swimming pool and *putting green* as well as tennis courts, squash courts and saunas.
5   (Peebles) . . . This *homely* hotel has been extended and renovated . . .
6   (Perth) . . . the Tay Valley and the nearby mountains, moors, lochs and *glens*.
7   (Pitlochry) . . . a delightful *resort* set amidst spectacular highland scenery.
8   (Pitlochry) . . . noted for its fine food and well-stocked *cellar*, . . .

B : MEANINGS

a) playing fields
b) exciting
c) place where you can play some kind of game
d) very small
e) place where wine is kept
f) is better than
g) narrow, lonely valleys
h) relaxing and energy-giving
i) place where people go on holiday
j) city
k) measures of land area
l) simple, not elegant
m) has a view over

Aviemore. Post House
There are superb views of the Cairngorms from this comfortable modern hotel, ideally placed for making the most of the wide choice of sports and entertainments available at Aviemore, Scotland's foremost year-round resort.

Edinburgh. Post House
A popular base for visitors to Edinburgh, this fine hotel stands next to the Zoological Gardens within easy reach of the many famous sights, shops and entertainments of one of Europe's most elegant capitals.

Gatehouse of Fleet. Cally Hotel∗
This impressive hotel, well-known for its good Scottish cooking, is an ideal choice for a relaxing family holiday. Set in 100 acres of private grounds, the Cally, a former stately home, has something for everyone including its own fishing loch, outdoor heated swimming pool, putting green, croquet lawn, tennis court, children's playground and sauna baths.

Glenborrodale. Glenborrodale Castle Hotel
There can be few better places for a refreshing holiday than this picturesque hotel set in its own 120 acres of beautiful rugged countryside by tranquil Loch Sunart on the Ardnamurchan Peninsular. Pony trekking June-September, boating and trout fishing are both available here.
Closed Nov. to March.

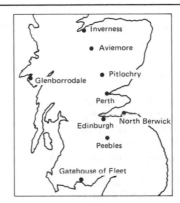

Inverness. Royal Hotel
A unique feature of the Royal is its fine collection of antique furniture, china and glass. This friendly comfortable hotel, a favourite meeting place for the townspeople, is an excellent base for getting to know the Highlands – Loch Ness, Great Glen and Culloden Moor are all within an easy drive.

North Berwick. Marine Hotel
This fine hotel overlooks the famous West Links golf course and the Firth of Forth and is close to several sandy beaches. The Marine has its own open-air swimming pool and putting green as well as tennis courts, squash courts and saunas. Some of Scotland's finest golf courses are in the area and Edinburgh is only some 24 miles away.

Peebles. Tontine Hotel
The Tontine had an intriguing beginning – it was built in 1808 by subscription, hence its name. This homely hotel has been extended and renovated to make it a really comfortable base for exploring the Tweed Valley and the attractive Lowland country.

Perth. Royal George Hotel
From the terrace of the Royal George there are magnificent views of the River Tay and Perth Bridge with the wooded slopes of Kinnoul Hill in the background. The hotel, restyled and modernised, is an excellent base for touring the Tay Valley and the nearby mountains, moors, lochs and glens.

Pitlochry. Atholl Palace Hotel∗
There's something for all the family at Pitlochry, a delightful resort set amidst spectacular Highland scenery. This imposing hotel, noted for its fine food and well-stocked cellar, has its own swimming pool, as well as tennis courts, saunas, a games room and pitch-and-putt course. Riding, fishing, golfing and boating are all available nearby.

Prices per person Prices per person are based on sharing a twin room with bath. Single room supplements with bath are shown next to the main prices.

There are no single room supplements during Winter.

Season & duration	Spring, Summer & Autumn ... **7** nights price						Winter... **5** nights price
Price includes	Accommodation, full traditional breakfast, three-course dinner with coffee, service and VAT						Winter prices also include lunch
Dates available	1st May-7th June		8th June-30th Sept		1st Oct-1st Nov		2nd Nov '81- 28th April '82
Town, hotel & telephone	Prices £s	Single Supp.	Prices £s	Single Supp.	Prices £s	Single Supp.	Prices £s
Aviemore Post House (0479) 810771	140.00	None	168.00	None	140.00	None	105.00
Edinburgh Post House 031-334 8221	129.50	None	171.50	None	129.50	None	112.50
Gatehouse of Fleet Cally Hotel (05574) 341	148.75	None	180.25	None	148.75	None	115.00
Glenborrodale Glenborrodale Castle (09724) 266 ∗	175.00	None	175.00	None	175.00	None	112.50
Inverness Royal Hotel (0463) 30665	143.50	None	143.50	None	143.50	None	100.00
North Berwick Marine Hotel (0620) 2406 ●	178.50	None	178.50	None	178.50	None	112.50
Peebles Tontine Hotel (0721) 20892	136.50	None	136.50	None	136.50	None	92.50
Perth Royal George Hotel (0738) 24455	168.00	None	168.00	None	168.00	None	100.00
Pitlochry Atholl Palace Hotel (0796) 2400	150.50	None	173.25	None	150.50	None	117.50

Children's Prices! see page 6

Winter Special ! 13 nights ·· £220 at all hotels

Notes: ∗Rooms without private bathroom are available at reduced prices ●Superior sea view rooms attract a supplement of £3.00 per person per night
Lunch option: Lunch inclusive prices are available at all hotels for Spring, Summer & Autumn

Shorter or longer holidays – see page 6 for full details – Spring, Summer & Autumn minimum 4 days, Winter minimum 3 days **How to book** – see back page

(From an advertisement for Trust House Forte Hotels.)

Cairngorms: a mountain range.   *Highlands*: mountainous country in Northern Scotland.
loch (Scottish): 1 lake; 2 arm of the sea, nearly surrounded by land.

Unit 8   Zen and the art of motorcycle maintenance

This text is the beginning of the first chapter in an American novel. Every 15 lines or so you will find a short summary of what you have just read. But the summary has mistakes in it! Put a line through the mistaken words or phrases in the summary and write the correct ones; or, on a separate piece of paper, write down the mistakes and corrections.

  Example: This is the ~~last~~ *first* part of a novel.

I can see by my watch, without taking my hand from the left grip of the cycle, that it is eight-thirty in the morning. The wind, even at sixty miles an hour, is warm and humid. When it's this hot and muggy at eight-thirty, I'm wondering what it's going to be like in the afternoon.   5

　　In the wind are pungent odors from the marshes by the road. We are in an area of the Central Plains filled with thousands of duck hunting sloughs, heading northwest from Minneapolis toward the Dakotas.   10
This highway is an old concrete two-laner that hasn't had much traffic since a four-laner went in parallel to it several years ago. When we pass a marsh the air suddenly becomes cooler. Then, when we are past, it suddenly warms up again.   15

Summary

The narrator is travelling across an area of the Rocky Mountains by

motorcycle. It is a hot, dry morning, and there are a lot of hills along the wide

new highway the narrator is using. The air from the marshes is warm.

　　I'm happy to be riding back into this country. It is a kind of nowhere, famous for nothing at all and has an appeal because of just that. Tensions disappear along old roads like this. We bump along the beat-up concrete between the cattails and stretches of meadow and   20
then more cattails and marsh grass. Here and there is a

---

odors: smells.
marshes: areas of low, wet, soft land.
concrete: building material used for road surfaces.

meadow: grassland.
narrator: the person who says 'I' in the story.

38

stretch of open water and if you look closely you **can**
see wild ducks at the edge of the cattails. And turtles.
. . . There's a red-winged blackbird.

I whack Chris's knee and point to it.   25

"What!" he hollers.

"Blackbird!"

He says something I don't hear. "What?" I holler
back.

He grabs the back of my helmet and hollers up,   30
"I've seen *lots* of those, Dad!"

Summary

This is the first time the narrator has been in this country. He is unhappy to be
back in this irritating place and see the plants and animals again. His son Chris,
who is riding beside him on another cycle, is impressed with the bird his dad
notices.

"Oh!" I holler back. Then I nod. At age eleven
you don't get very impressed with red-winged blackbirds.

You have to get older for that. For me this is all   35
mixed with memories that he doesn't have. Cold morn-
ings long ago when the marsh grass had turned brown
and cattails were waving in the northwest wind. The
pungent smell then was from muck stirred up by hip
boots while we were getting in position for the sun to   40
come up and the duck season to open. Or winters when
the sloughs were frozen over and dead and I could walk
across the ice and snow between the dead cattails and
see nothing but grey skies and dead things and cold.
The blackbirds were gone then. But now in July they're 45
back and everything is at its alivest and every foot of
these sloughs is humming and cricking and buzzing
and chirping, a whole community of millions of living
things living out their lives in a kind of benign con-
tinuum.   50

Summary

Chris is 11; the narrator thinks that is too old to be impressed with blackbirds.
The blackbird is interesting to the narrator because it reminds him of a story he
read: deer hunting in the marshes in the autumn, walking through the mud in
the winter.

---

benign: having a kind or gentle nature.

You see things vacationing on a motorcycle in a way that is completely different from any other. In a car you're always in a compartment, and because you're used to it you don't realize that through that car window everything you see is just more TV. You're a passive observer and it is all moving by you boringly in a frame.   55

On a cycle the frame is gone. You're completely in contact with it all. You're *in* the scene, not just watching it anymore, and the sense of presence is overwhelming. That concrete whizzing by five inches below your foot is the real thing, the same stuff you walk on, it's right there, so blurred you can't focus on it, yet you can put your foot down and touch it anytime, and the whole thing, the whole experience, is never removed   65 from immediate consciousness.   60

Chris and I are traveling to Montana with some friends riding up ahead, and maybe headed farther than that. Plans are deliberately indefinite, more to travel than to arrive anywhere. We are just vacationing.   70

(From *Zen and the art of motorcycle maintenance* by Robert M. Pirsig.)

Summary

Travelling on a motorcycle is not so good as travelling by car because on a motorcycle you are a participant rather than a spectator. You can ignore the experience of travelling. The narrator and his son have very definite plans about their vacation, because it is the destination that interests them more than the journey.

blurred: when something is blurred you cannot see it clearly.
deliberately: intentionally.

Have you got the main ideas?

Which three of the following subjects do you think the author is most interested in discussing in this passage?
– How to hunt ducks.
– The scenery.
– The narrator's relationship with his son Chris.
– The narrator's past experience of this place.
– The pleasure and interest of travelling by motorcycle.
– The weather.
– Chris's attitude to nature.

Guessing unknown words

Find *single* words in the text which seem to correspond to the definitions given below.

Example   (in lines 1–5):
              The part of a motorcycle that you hold in your hand when the cycle
              is moving.
Answer: grip

Now find words for these meanings in lines 1–25:
1 A muddy place where people go to hunt ducks.
2 A road wide enough for one car going in each direction.
3 Wet, close, heavy (referring to the weather).
4 Plants that grow in wet places, whose flowers look like cats' tails.
5 Move over a rough road, for example in a car or on a cycle.

Find words for these meanings in lines 26–50:
6 Sticky mud mixed with decaying plants.
7 The protective hat a motorcyclist wears.
8 Shouts.

Find words for these meanings in lines 51–70:
9   Adjust your eyes (or a camera) so the image is clear.
10 Speeding.
11 Making you weak with emotion.

Part 3 Processes: How things happen

Unit 9 Drinking while driving – how does the test work?

Here is a text about British police tests for the amount of alcohol a driver has drunk. Read the text slowly, twice. Pause as often as you wish. Imagine you will have to make a summary of the text.

Then do the exercises. Do not worry if you cannot answer all the questions without referring to the text. This is normal: the exercises are to teach you, not test you.

Anybody can be asked to take the first stage of the test. Any driver stopped by the police for a normal caution arising out of some quite minor traffic infringement (such as crossing a white line), any driver involved in an accident (whether it's his fault or not) or any driver whom the police suspect has been drinking can be asked to take the test.   5

Stage 1. At the roadside the driver will be asked to blow through a small glass tube into a plastic bag. Inside the tube are chemically treated crystals which change colour if the driver has alcohol on his breath. If the colour change goes beyond a certain line marked on the tube this indicates that the driver is probably over the specified limit. If the colour change does not reach the line the driver is in the clear   10
under the new law. But if the colour change *does* reach the line then the test has proved positive and the driver will be asked to go to the police station for . . .

Stage 2. At the police station the driver can repeat the first test — the one he has already taken at the roadside — if he wants to. This check is for his protection. But if he does not take a second breath test, or if the second test also proves positive, he   15
goes on to . . .

Stage 3. Still at the police station, the driver is required to give a sample of blood. This is provided quite painlessly by pricking a finger or the lobe of an ear. If the driver refuses a blood sample he is required to give two samples of urine within one hour. After this, the driver can leave immediately provided he is not going to drive.   20
If he *is* going to drive he will be detained in the station until the police are satisfied he is below the limit.

Stage 4. The driver's blood or urine samples are sent to the forensic laboratories where they are analysed by the latest scientific equipment. If the analysis shows that the driver has more than 80 milligrammes of alcohol in every 100 millilitres of his   25
blood then the driver has broken the law and will be prosecuted.

It is the evidence of this analysis which the police will use in court and once the blood alcohol level has been established there is no room for argument.

But the driver does have this reassurance: At Stage 3 (see above) he can ask for an extra sample of his blood or urine, taken at the same time. He can send this sample   30
to a doctor of his own choice for independent analysis. In this, as in the opportunity to take a second breath test, the driver's rights are protected twice over and every care is taken to eliminate the chance of error.

A driver convicted as a result of the test will be disqualified from driving for one year. The fact that he needs his licence to make his living — as a lorry-driver,   35
salesman or doctor for example — will make no difference. But a doctor who is called out to an emergency on a night when he is not 'on call', could plead that there was a special and inescapable reason why he had to drive when over the limit.

Under the new law the courts can take a very few such 'special reasons' into account.
40

As well as disqualification a convicted driver may also be fined up to £100 or he may be sent to prison for up to four months — or both.

(From *The new law on drink and driving*, H.M.S.O.)

caution: warning

Summary skills 1

Complete this diagram of the first three stages of the test.

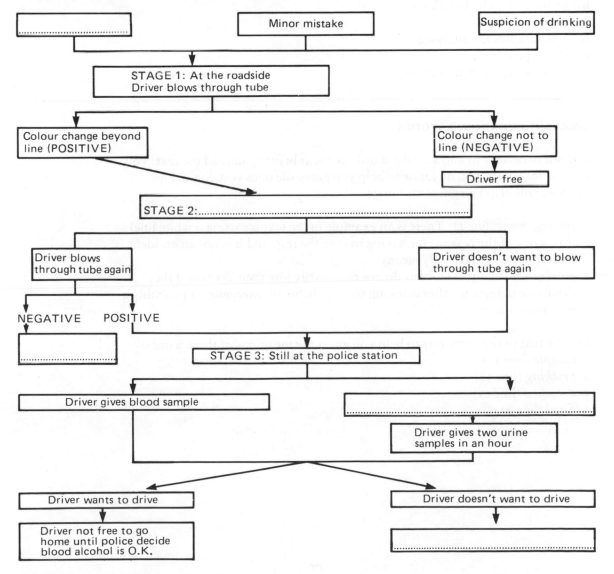

Summary skills 2

Write the numbers 1 to 9 on a piece of paper, for the nine paragraphs in the text. Then choose a title for each paragraph from the list below. Be careful: there are three extra titles.

a) A second breath test is possible.
b) Disqualification.
c) Refusing to give blood samples.
d) Protection of driver's rights.
e) Blood or urine samples are taken.
f) Who takes the test?
g) Doctors and 'special reasons'.
h) At the roadside: breath test.
i) Colour changes.
j) The samples are analysed.
k) Other penalties.
l) Laboratory evidence is final.

Guessing unknown words

It is not necessary to know all the words in a text before you read the text: you can use the words you *do* know to help you guess the ones you don't. This exercise will help you guess meanings.

1 *infringement* (line 2): There is an example in the text (crossing a white line): this is one of the reasons for having to take the test, and it is not an accident. So *infringement* probably means ....
2 *emergency* (line 37): Doctors do not necessarily lose their licences if they drive to emergencies after drinking too much. So an *emergency* is probably a situation where ....

Use the text in the same way to help you guess the meanings of these words:
3 *sample* (line 17)
4 *pricking* (line 18)
5 *detained* (line 21)
6 *fined* (line 41)

Unit 10   Drinks from fruits and grains

Reading for specific information

Complete the following table with information from the passage on the next page. Make sure you check your answers with the text! The column headed *Red wine* is done as an example.

	Red wine	White wine	Beer	Port	Gin	Scotch whisky	Brandy
Made from dark grapes	X						
Made from white grapes							
Made from grain							
Must be drunk quickly	X						
Can be drunk long after it is opened							
Contains no distilled alcohol	X						
Contains some distilled alcohol							
Made completely of distilled alcohol							

Early in the development of agriculture men discovered how to make alcoholic drinks from grapes and corn. The ancient Egyptians drank both wine and beer, and the Greeks carried on a lively trade in wine throughout the Mediterranean. The vines of grapes are all of a single species, *Vitis vinifera*, although there are hundreds of varieties   5
adapted to different soils and climates.

Wine is the fermented juice of fresh grapes. The juice of the wine grape contains sugar, and growths of yeast form on the outside of the grape skins. In wine-making, the grapes are crushed in a wine press and the yeast converts the sugar to alcohol, when there is no air   10
present, by a process called fermentation. Red wine is made from dark grapes, and white wine from white grapes or from dark grapes whose skins have been removed from the wine press at an early stage. The most famous wine-growing countries are France, Germany and Italy. Wine was made in England in the Middle Ages, but the climate   15
is not really suitable for grapevines. Wines must be drunk quickly once they are opened, otherwise bacteria will use the air to convert the alcohol to vinegar. The bacteria are killed by a higher alcohol content than is found in wine and that is why sherry and port, the specialties of Spain and Portugal, are fortified by the addition of   20
spirits to make them last longer.

Beer is made from sprouting barley grains (malt) which is fermented with yeast to produce alcohol; hops are added for flavour. Ale, the most common drink in England in the Middle Ages, was also made from barley, but without hops; the ale of today is merely a   25
type of beer. In Japan beer is made from rice.

Spirits have a higher alcoholic content than beer and wine and are made by distillation from a base of grain or some other vegetable. Gin and vodka can be distilled from a variety of ingredients, including potatoes; gin is flavoured with juniper berries. Scotch whisky is   30
obtained from a base of fermented barley, and brandy from the distillation of wine. Rum is derived from sugar cane by fermentation of molasses, a by-product in refining sugar. Cider is made from apples. South American Indians make alcoholic drinks from cactus leaves and the shoots of certain palm trees.   35

(From *The Penguin book of the natural world*)

sprouting: beginning to grow.
barley: a grain plant, of the same family as wheat and oats.
hops: seed-cases of a certain flowering plant.
distillation: the process in which a liquid is heated to make a gas, then cooled to make a liquid
  again.

Guessing unknown words

You have already done exercises to guess the meaning of words you do not
know. You know that understanding the words in a text does not necessarily
mean being able to give a dictionary definition of each word. For example, if
you had never seen the word 'yeast' (line 8) before, several things would help
you to understand it:
– You know from its form and from its place in the sentence that it is a noun.
– You know that it grows on the outside of grape skins, so it is probably some
   kind of simple plant.
– You know that it converts sugar to alcohol.
– You know that this is what changes grape juice to wine and barley to beer.
Most native speakers of English probably do not know any more about yeast
than you do. What you know is quite sufficient for understanding the word in
the text.
   Now look at the text, and use what you find to give probable answers to these
questions.

1 A simpler word for *species* (line 5) is ....
2 What does a *wine press* (lines 9–10) do?
3 A *juniper* (line 30) is some sort of ....
4 A simpler word for *derived* (line 32) is ....
5 A *shoot* (line 35) is part of ....

Inference

Sometimes you can find information in a text that is not stated clearly by the
words there. You infer the information – that is, you make a logical guess –
either from what is in the text, or by using your knowledge of the world, or
both.
   Try to infer the probable answers to these questions by looking at the text; be
ready to give your reasons.

1 Do we know exactly when and where beer was invented?
2 Can fermentation take place if air is present?
3 What gives the colour to red wine?
4 Is ale the most common drink in England today?
5 There are different kinds of whisky: Scotch whisky, Irish whiskey, Canadian
   whiskey, Bourbon whiskey .... Are they all made from barley?

Unit 11   The town that kids built

Read this American text about an unusual sort of school programme. Be sure to read the text slowly, twice; and then do the exercises that follow. It is perfectly all right to look back at the text while doing the exercises.

"My children really understand solar power and geothermal energy," says a second-grade teacher in Saugus, California. "Some of them are building solar collectors and turbines for their energy course." These young scientists are part of City Building Educational Program, a unique curriculum for kindergarten through twelfth grade that uses the process of city planning to teach basic reading, writing, and math skills, and more.

The children don't just plan any city. They map and analyze the housing, energy, and transportation requirements of their own community and project its needs in 100 years. With the help of an architect consultant who visits the classroom once a week, they invent new ways to meet these needs and build Styrofoam models of their creations. "Designing buildings of the future gives children a lot of freedom," says Doreen Nelson, the teacher who developed this program. "They are able to use their own space-age fantasies and inventions without fear of criticism, because there are no wrong answers in a future context. In fact, as the class enters the final model-building phase of the program, an elected 'mayor' and 'planning commission' make all the design decisions for the model city, and the teacher steps back and becomes an adviser."

CBEP is a series of activities, games, and simulations that teach the basic steps necessary for problem-solving: observing, analyzing, creating possible solutions, and evaluating them based on the children's own criteria. Here are some highlights of the program.

The children draw free-form maps of their town and analyze what's "good" and "bad" about it ("the freeway is good because it helps you get places fast, and bad because it produces noise and pollution") to decide what they want in their future city.

To understand the way that towns are organized so that people can deal with the natural environment, the children create an imaginary landscape out of Styrofoam with mountains, rivers, meadows, and forests; they then pretend they're in primitive times. Shelters are constructed. One child, using a hair dryer, pretends to be the wind; another with a lamp is the sun; and another simulates rain with a water pistol. Those shelters that are too close to the river are washed away in a flood. Afterward, the children discuss their mistakes. In a second version, they may organise into tribes for survival and division of labor. With each simulation they get better at surviving.

In another preliminary exercise for redesigning their town, the children analyze their classroom environment by using a scale model of the room with miniature desks and chairs. Each child presents her or his plan to a small group. Then the most successful plan is chosen and set up in the classroom. This helps the children think of their class as a community, and gives them some control over what is happening in the classroom. It also teaches them the way people can be organized to create and implement a plan that improves the environment. The children also work with the classroom as if it were a city — with aisles as highways, desks as houses, bookcases as the library/cultural center.

A group develops a plan for subdividing the site of their future city into land parcels, using hills, streams, and other features as natural boundaries. Areas are marked off for housing, industry, and open space, and the parcels are distributed to all the

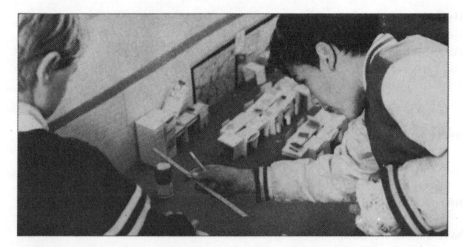

students. Then the children try out different forms of government — monarchy, dictatorship, democracy — in order to choose one for the planning phase of the city. They elect a ruler who appoints a planning commission to make the final design decisions for each building in the future city.

90   94

(From an article by Phyllis Rosser in *Ms*.)

second grade: the second year of elementary school in the United States: Children in the second grade are about seven years old.
curriculum: programme of studies.
Styrofoam: a light plastic material that can easily be cut into different shapes.

Summary skills 1

Choose the four most important points from this list and put them in a logical order. This can be the same order as you find the ideas in the text, or a different order, as long as it is logical. Compare your answers with other students and see if you have found more than one logical order.

a) The children learn about solar power and geothermal energy in order to build solar collectors and turbines.
b) The children have a lot of freedom to design their community in the way they want.
c) CBEP includes several preparatory exercises leading to the building of a model of a future town.
d) The children try out different forms of government in order to choose one for the planning phase of the city.
e) The children participating in the programme make a detailed plan for meeting the needs of their own town or city.
f) The children draw maps of their town and analyze them to see what is good and bad about each aspect of the community.
g) CBEP uses the process of city planning to teach both ordinary school subjects and the general skill of problem-solving.

Summary skills 2

Here are some general statements about CBEP. For each statement, give as
many details as you can (examples, reasons, results, specific descriptions, etc.)
Include only details directly related to each statement.
Example: An architect comes to the class room.
Some details:
The architect comes once a week.
He or she
— advises the children;
— helps them invent ways of solving problems;
— helps them construct models of future buildings.

1 The children have a lot of freedom.
2 The children pretend they are in primitive times.
3 The children rearrange their classroom.
4 The children subdivide their city.

Guessing unknown words

Here is an exercise to help you guess unknown words. Match each italicized
word in column A with the meaning in column B that comes closest to it.
Column B has some extra meanings.

COLUMN A

1 'In fact, as the class enters the final model-building
   phase of the program, an elected 'mayor' and
   'planning commission' make all the design decisions.'
   (line 28)
2 'They are able to use their own *space-age* fantasies
   and inventions without fear of criticism, because
   there are no wrong answers in a future context.'
   (line 24)
3 They may organize into *tribes* for survival and
   division of labour. (line 60)
4 The children draw *free-form* maps of their town and
   analyze what's 'good' and 'bad' about it. (line 40)
5 A group develops a plan for subdividing the site of
   their future city into land *parcels*, using hills, streams,
   and other features as natural boundaries. (line 82)
6 The children also work with the classroom as if it
   were a city – with *aisles* as highways, desks as houses,
   bookcases as the library / cultural center. (line 78)
7 They elect a ruler who *appoints* a planning
   commission to make the final design decisions ...
   (line 91)

COLUMN B

a) not precise
b) small areas
c) futuristic
d) passages between rows of
    seats
e) a period or part in a series
    of events
f) proposes as candidates
g) chooses and names
h) groups of people who live
    close together and share work
    and food
i) corridors joining one
    classroom to another
j) boxes

Accurate comprehension

Mark each sentence with **T** if it is true according to the text, **F** if it is false according to the text, and **DS** if the text doesn't say.

1 The City Building Educational Program is only used with older children.
2 The children's final project is to plan a completely imaginary city.
3 The children study their own city in its present state before planning a future city.
4 When the architect comes, the children meet with her or him in small groups.
5 The children do the 'primitive times' simulation only once.
6 In one exercise the children pretend their classroom is a city.

Unit 12   Inside story

This is the last text in this part. The ideas in it are more difficult than those in the other texts. Use the same techniques for understanding it as before: read it twice, slowly. Pause in reading as often as you want to. Imagine that you will have to make a summary of the text: this will help you to read more efficiently.

Then do the exercises that follow the text, looking back at the text as often as you need to.

When you close your eyes and try to think of the shape of your own body, what you imagine (or, rather, what you
5 feel) is quite different from what you see when you open your eyes and look in the mirror. The image you feel is much vaguer than the one you
10 see. And if you lie still, it is quite hard to imagine yourself as having any particular size or shape.

When you move, when you
15 feel the weight of your arms and legs and the natural resistance of the objects around you, the 'felt' image of yourself starts to become clearer. It is
20 almost as if it were created by your own actions and the sensations they cause.

The image you create for yourself has rather strange
25 proportions: certain parts feel much larger than they look. If you poke your tongue into a hole in one of your teeth, it feels enormous; you are often
30 surprised by how small it looks when you inspect it in the mirror.

But although the 'felt' image may not have the shape you
35 see in the mirror, it is much more important. It is the image through which you recognise your physical existence in the world. In spite of its strange proportions, it is all one piece, 40 and since it has a consistent right and left and top and bottom, it allows you to locate new sensations when they occur. It allows you to find your 45 nose in the dark, scratch itches and point to a pain.

If the felt image is damaged for any reason—if it is cut in half or lost, as it often is after 50 certain strokes which wipe out recognition of one entire side —these tasks become almost impossible. What is more, it becomes hard to make sense of 55 one's own visual appearance. If one half of the felt image is wiped out or injured, the patient stops recognising the affected part of his body. It is 60 hard for him to find the location of sensations on that side, and, although he feels the doctor's touch, he locates it as being on the undamaged side. 65

He loses his ability to accept the affected side as part of his body, even when he can see it. If you throw him a pair of gloves and ask him to put 70 them on, he will glove one hand and leave the other bare.

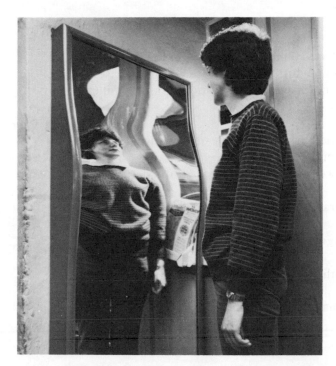

And yet he had to use the left hand in order to glove the right. The fact that he can see the ungloved hand doesn't seem to help him, and there is no reason why it should. He can no longer reconcile what he sees with what he feels—the ungloved object lying on the left may look like a hand, but, since there is no felt image corresponding to it, why should he claim the object as his?

(Adapted from an article by Dr Jonathan Miller in the *Guardian*.)

stroke: a sudden reduction of the blood supply to a part of the brain, often causing loss of feeling and power in part of the body.

Have you got the main ideas?

Mark each sentence with **T** if it is true according to the text, and **F** if it is false according to the text.

1 The image of your body you feel with your eyes closed is different and less clear than the image you can see in a mirror.
2 You feel as if the weight of your arms and legs were created by your own actions.
3 The 'felt' image is much larger than the 'mirror' image.
4 The 'felt' image is important because it lets you know in what part of your body you are feeling something.
5 Certain strokes eliminate half of the felt image.
6 Some patients who have had strokes cannot see one side of their bodies.

Families of words

Part of our understanding of a text is based on recognition of families of words – which word means the same as another word, which word is a more precise way of saying the same thing, and so on. Answer these questions about families of words.

1 Find a word in the first paragraph that gives an example of how the felt image is *different* (line 5) from the mirror image.
2 *Sensations* (lines 21–22): Find two words in the second paragraph describing things that you sense.
3 Find three words in the third paragraph that give information about *proportions* (line 25).
4 Find three words in the fourth paragraph that are other ways of saying *locate* (line 43).
5 Find three words or expressions in the fifth paragraph that are other ways of saying *damaged* (line 48).
6 Find a word in the last paragraph that means the same as *bare* (line 72).

What does *it* mean?

Look at this sentence:

> But although the 'felt' image may not have the shape you see in the mirror, *it* is much more important.

To understand the sentence, you must realize that *it* means 'the "felt" image'. If you think that *it* means 'the shape' or 'the mirror', you will have trouble following the rest of the text. This is not a very difficult skill, but it needs practice. Practise it by answering the questions below. Give the meaning of each italicized *it*. (The meaning can be in the same sentence as *it* or elsewhere in the text.)

1 It is almost as if *it* were created by your own actions . . . (line 20)
2 If you poke your tongue into a hole in one of your teeth, *it* feels enormous; . . . (line 28)
3 In spite of *its* strange proportions, it is all one piece, . . . (line 39)
4 If the felt image is damaged for any reason – if *it* is cut in half or lost, . . . (line 49)
5 It is hard for him to find the location of sensations on that side, and although he feels the doctor's touch, he locates *it* as being on the undamaged side. (line 64)
6 He loses his ability to accept the affected side as part of his body, even when he can see *it*. (line 68)
7 The fact that he can see the ungloved hand doesn't seem to help him, and there is no reason why *it* should. (line 78)
8 . . . the ungloved object lying on the left may look like a hand, but, since there is no felt image corresponding to *it*, why should he claim the object as his? (line 84)

Inference

What evidence is there in the text for the following?

Example: After the strokes Dr Miller writes about, people have trouble putting their shoes on.

Answer: *After these strokes, people will only put on one of a pair of gloves; so they probably have the same problem with shoes.*

1 Details of the 'felt' image can change quite often.
2 People who are paralysed have very vague images of themselves.
3 The strokes Dr Miller writes about do not paralyse.
4 The strokes Dr Miller writes about do not destroy feeling in the affected part of the body.
5 You can't always correct the 'felt' image by looking at yourself.

Part 4   Narrative: What happened

Unit 13   The diamond

This is part of a short story. Read it carefully, more than once if you wish, before doing the exercises.

There was a man called Ephraim who lived in Johannesburg. His father was to do with diamonds, as had been his father. The family were immigrants. This is still true of all people from Johannesburg, a city a century old. Ephraim was a middle son, not brilliant or stupid, not good or bad. He was nothing in particular. His brothers became diamond merchants, but Ephraim was not cut out for anything immediately obvious, and so at last he was apprenticed to an uncle to learn the trade of diamond-cutting.   5

To cut a diamond perfectly is an act like a samurai's sword-thrust, or a master archer's centred arrow. When an important diamond is shaped a man may spend a week, or even weeks, studying it, accumulating powers of attention, memory, intuition, till he has reached that moment when he finally knows that a tap, no more, at just *that* point of tension in the stone will split it exactly *so*.   10   15

While Ephraim learned to do this, he lived at home in a Johannesburg suburb; and his brothers and sisters married and had families. He was the son who took his time about getting married, and about whom the family first joked, saying that he was choosy; and then they remained silent when others talked of him with that edge on their voices, irritated, a little malicious, even frightened, which is caused by those men and women who refuse to fulfil the ordinary purposes of nature. The kind ones said he was a good son, working nicely under his uncle Ben, and living respectably at home, and on Sunday nights playing poker with bachelor friends. He was twenty-five, then thirty, thirty-five, forty. His parents became old and died, and he lived alone in the family house. People stopped noticing him. Nothing was expected of him.   20   25   30

Then a senior person became ill, and Ephraim was asked to fly in his stead to Alexandria for a special job. A certain rich merchant of Alexandria had purchased an uncut diamond as a present for his daughter, who was to be married shortly. He wished only the best for the diamond. Ephraim, revealed by this happening as one of the world's master diamond-cutters, flew to Egypt, spent some days in communion with the stone in a quiet room in the merchant's house, and then caused it to fall apart into three lovely pieces. These were for a ring and earrings.   35

Now he should have flown home again; but the merchant asked him to dinner. An odd chance that – unusual. Not many   40 people got inside that rich closed world. But perhaps the merchant had become infected by the week of rising tension while Ephraim became one with the diamond in a quiet room.

    At dinner Ephraim met the girl for whom the jewels were destined.   45

(From 'Out of the fountain' by Doris Lessing.)

thrust: a sudden, forceful push.

Summary skills

Write the numbers 1 to 6 on a piece of paper, for the six paragraphs in the story. Then choose the best title for each paragraph from this list, and write the title letter next to the paragraph number. Be careful: there are ten titles in all, but you will only need six.

a) The art of diamond cutting
b) The girl
c) Rising tension
d) Invitation to dinner
e) Ephraim becomes a diamond cutter
f) A time-consuming job
g) A city of immigrants
h) Ephraim's family
i) An unexpected job
j) Single and middle-aged

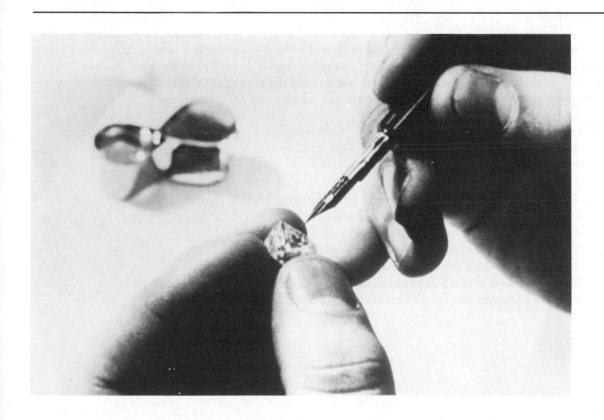

Making connections

Misunderstandings sometimes happen because we do not realize what is meant by a word like *she* or *it*. This exercise will give you practice in making the connections between these words and their meanings. Give the meaning of each word in italics. (The meaning can be in the same sentence or elsewhere in the text.)

Example: *He* was nothing in particular.
Answer: *He* means *Ephraim*.

1   His father was to do with diamonds, as had been *his father*. (line 2)
2   While Ephraim learned to do *this*, he lived at home in a Johannesburg suburb; ... (line 17)
3   The kind *ones* said he was a good son, ... (line 24)
4   Then a senior person became ill, and Ephraim was asked to fly in *his* stead to Alexandria for a special job. (line 32)
5   Ephraim, revealed by this happening as one of the world's master diamond-cutters, flew to Egypt, spent some days in communion with the stone in a quiet room in the merchant's house, and then caused *it* to fall apart into three lovely pieces. (line 38)

Inference

It is important to understand what a text says, and what it suggests. It is also important *not* to think a story says or suggests more than it does. Try to do this exercise without looking back at the text; but do read the text again if the exercise begins to seem too difficult. Just answer yes or no to each question.

Does the text say:
1   How many brothers Ephraim had?
2   What Ephraim's brothers did?
3   Who Ephraim worked for?
4   How long Ephraim was an apprentice before cutting his first diamond?
5   Whether Ephraim had any nephews or nieces?
6   Where Ephraim was living when he was sent to Egypt?
7   Whether Ephraim's friends thought he would become famous?
8   How many children the rich merchant had?
9   Where Ephraim was when he cut the diamond?
10 Whether Ephraim met the girl before cutting the diamond?

Opinions and feelings

In this story, the author communicates opinions and feelings – her own and her characters' – by telling the reader what the characters did. This exercise will help you think about those ideas and feelings. Match each phrase in column A with its best description in column B. There are some extra descriptions in column B.

COLUMN A

1 Ephraim as a child
2 A professional diamond cutter
3 How Ephraim's not getting married made some people feel
4 Ephraim's private life in Johannesburg
5 Ephraim's ability to cut diamonds
6 Ephraim's approach to cutting the rich merchant's diamond
7 The rich merchant, observing Ephraim's way of working

COLUMN B

a) difficult
b) impressed
c) uninteresting
d) unexceptional
e) mystical
f) highly skilled
g) exceptional
h) bored
i) violent
j) uncomfortable

Unit 14   Dear editors

This letter was printed in a psychology magazine. Read it carefully before doing the exercises.

Dear Editors,

Your readers may be interested in the following account of the behaviour modification of a small girl.

Kathy started at my nursery school at the age of two years nine months. She was small for her age but confident, competent and determined. She settled into the group easily, would be first on the slide and highest up the climbing frame. She could put on her coat without help and not only fasten her own buttons but fasten other children's too.

She was a lovely child but unfortunately a scratcher. If anyone upset her or stood in her way her right hand would flash out faster than Mohammed Ali's and score down the face of her playmates from forehead to chin. Children twice her age would fly in terror from her and cower screaming in corners.

This must have been very rewarding for Kathy but obviously it had to be stopped – and stopped quickly. All the usual ways failed and then I remembered an account by G. C. E. Atkinson of Highfield School, Haledown, Liverpool of how bullying in the playground had been stopped.

No punishment had been given, but the bullies had been ignored and the victims rewarded. So I decided that in future Kathy would be ignored and her victim given a sweet.

With a pocketful of Smarties I followed Kathy around. She was so quick that it was impossible to prevent her scratching but I was determined to stay within arms length all afternoon.

All was peaceful but then I saw Kathy's hand descend and heard the scream. Quickly and gently I gathered up the little hurt one and cradling her in my arms said 'Nice, nice sweetie' and I popped it into her mouth. Kathy opened her mouth expectantly and then when she got nothing looked puzzled.

Minutes later another scream, this time from John and while cuddling him I said 'Look Kathy, a nice Smartie for John' and put the sweet into John's open mouth.

A smile of understanding flashed across Kathy's face and holding a finger

tenderly came to me and
wailed 'Hurt my finger'.
   'Never mind' said I coldly
'It will soon be better'. She
85 stamped her small foot and
shouted *'Give me a
Smartie, I have hurt my
finger!'*
   'No' I replied, 'You'll get
90 a sweet if someone hurts
you'.
   Deliberately she turned
and scratched a child,
waited quietly while I
95 mothered and rewarded
him, then walked away.

She has never scratched a
child since.
   Parents who find older
children bullying younger   100
brothers and sisters might
do well to replace shouting
and punishment by
rewarding and giving more
attention to the injured one.   105
It's certainly less exhausting.

Margaret Seekree,
Belcombe Croft
Nursery School,
Bradford-on-Avon,   110
Wiltshire

(From *Psychology today*.)

bullying: a bully is someone who hurts people weaker than her or him.

Summary skills 1

Summarize the letter in one sentence.

Summary skills 2

Try to do this exercise without looking at the text; but do not hesitate to look
back at the text if the exercise is difficult.

   Write the numbers 1 to 13 down the side of a piece of paper. Then write the
letter of each event in the story, in the order it happened. Be careful: you will
need to use some letters more than once, because some events happened more
than once.

a) Kathy scratched a child.
b) Kathy opened her mouth for a sweet.
c) Kathy told the teacher her finger was hurt.
d) Kathy demanded a sweet.
e) Kathy stopped scratching.
f) The teacher ignored Kathy and gave the other child a sweet.
g) The teacher gave the other child a sweet and made sure Kathy noticed.
h) The teacher ignored Kathy.
i) The teacher answered Kathy without sympathy.

Guessing unknown words 1

1 Kathy was a scratcher. So in the phrase 'score down the face of her playmates,' (lines 25–26), *score* probably means ....

2 (line 70) Kathy was expecting a sweet and did not get one. A person who is *puzzled* is probably a person who does not ....

3 (line 82) Kathy was pretending her finger was hurt. So *wailed* probably means 'said in a .... way'.

Guessing unknown words 2

This is like the last exercise, but you will have less help. Choose the words you do not already know from this list and try to guess what they mean.

1 *forehead* (line 27): The forehead is at the .... of the face.

2 *rewarding* (line 32): Seeing the results of her scratching gave Kathy

....

3 *Smarties* (lines 51, 75, 87): This is a kind of ....

4 *cuddling* (line 73): You cuddle someone with your .... Some of the people you might cuddle are .... and ....

5 *exhausting* (line 106): Is it pleasant for something to be exhausting? .... You cannot guess exactly from the text, but exhausting might mean ....

Dividing sentences

Sometimes we misunderstand what we read because we divide long sentences incorrectly. This exercise will give you practice in dividing sentences.

For each sentence, decide whether there should be a division in the place marked. One way to decide might be to ask yourself: 'If I were saying the sentence, could I pause there?' There may be other divisions than the one marked.

Example 1:   Your readers may be interested in the following account of the behaviour / modification of a small girl.

Answer: No division. (*Behaviour* is a noun, but here it is used rather like an adjective, and belongs with *modification*.)

Example 2:   She could put on her coat without help / and not only fasten her own buttons but fasten other children's too.

Answer: Division. (*And* does not join *help* to *not*; *and* begins the second part of the sentence, telling what else Kathy could do.)

1 If anyone upset her or stood in her way / her right hand would flash out faster than Mohammed Ali's . . .

2 Children twice her age would fly in terror from her and cower / screaming in corners.

3 So I decided that in future Kathy would be ignored and her victim / given a sweet.
4 Quickly and gently I gathered up the little hurt one and / cradling her in my arms said 'Nice, nice sweetie' . . .
5 Kathy opened her mouth expectantly and then when she got nothing / looked puzzled.
6 Parents who find older children bullying younger brothers and sisters might do well to replace shouting and punishment by rewarding and giving / more attention to the injured one.

Accurate comprehension

For each sentence, write **T** if it is true according to the text, **F** if it is false according to the text, and **DS** if the text doesn't say.

1 Kathy was a difficult child in many ways.
2 Kathy was bigger than most of the other children.
3 Older children did not fight back when Kathy scratched them.
4 Margaret Seekree, who wrote the letter, got the idea from a teacher who had written an article in the same magazine.
5 Ms Seekree has also tried this method with her own child who bullied his younger brothers and sisters.

Unit 15   Great operatic disasters

These are the first two stories from a book about technical disasters during opera performances. Read them slowly, more than once if you like, before doing the exercises.

Tosca: *City Center, New York, 1960*

This catastrophe is due, not to misunderstanding and incompetence, but entirely to ill-will between the stage staff and the soprano. With diabolical
5 cunning they permitted her, after several stormy rehearsals, to complete her first performance without mishap until the very last moment, when Tosca throws herself off the battlements of the Castel Sant'Angelo. What normally happens is
10 that on her cry *'Scarpia, davanti a Dio'* she hurls herself off and lands on a mattress four feet below. This large young American singer landed not on a mattress, but – perish the thought – on a *trampoline*. It is said that she came up fifteen times before the curtain fell – sometimes upside down, 15 then the right way up – now laughing in delirious glee, now screaming with rage .... Worse still, it seems that the unhappy lady was unable to reappear in New York because the Center's faithful audience, remembering the trampoline, would 20 have burst into laughter. She had to remove herself to San Francisco, where of course no such grotesque incident could possibly occur ....

Tosca: *San Francisco Opera, 1961*

25 One must remember that *Tosca* is thought to be an 'easy' opera for a producer; there are in effect only three principals – Tosca, Cavaradossi and Scarpia. The other participants amount only to the first-act chorus (some rehearsal needed here),
30 the second-act choir (off stage thank God) and the third-act execution squad (no problem, they don't sing...). Alas, it is thus that fatal errors are engendered. On this particular occasion that innocuous firing squad was composed of
35 enthusiastic local college boys, totally ignorant of the story. As the dress rehearsal had to be cancelled because of illness, the execution squad appeared on the opening night only five minutes after their first and only consultation with the
40 producer. In a hurry, he had told them, 'O.K., boys. When the stage-manager cues you, slow-march in, wait until the officer lowers his sword, then shoot.' 'But how do we get off?' 'Oh – well, exit with the principals.' (This is the standard
45 American instruction for minor characters, servants, etc.)

The audience, therefore, saw the following: a group of soldiers marched on to the stage but stopped dead in its tracks at the sight of *two* 50 people, not one as they had assumed – a man and a woman, both looking extremely alarmed. They pointed their hesitant rifles at the man, but he started giving strange glances at the woman ... they pointed them at her, but she made a series of violently negative gestures – but then what 55 else would she do if she was about to be shot? The opera was called Tosca, it was evidently tragic, the enormous woman on stage was presumably Tosca herself, the officer was raising his sword 60

Thus it happened. *They shot Tosca instead of Cavaradossi.* To their amazement they then saw the man, some twenty yards away, fall lifeless to the ground, while the person they *had* shot rushed over to him. What could they do? They had shot 65 one of the principals – though admittedly the wrong one – and their next instruction was 'Exit with the principals'. Spoletta and his minions burst on to the stage and Tosca – could it be true? took up her position on top of the battle- 70 ments. She jumped, and there was only one thing for it – as the curtain slowly descended the whole firing-squad threw themselves after her ....

(Adapted from *Great Operatic Disasters* by Hugh Vickers.)

stage: the place in a theatre (usually at the front) where the actors perform.
trampoline:

execution squad: a group of soldiers who shoot a criminal condemned to death.
dress rehearsal: the last practice performance of an opera, with all the actors present in their costumes.

Summary skills 1

Here is a summary of the first story. Fill in the blanks with appropriate words.

In New York in 1960, the .... in *Tosca* was not very friendly with the .... workers. So instead of giving her a .... to fall on when she .... from the castle in the last act, they gave her a .... Instead of disappearing she .... up behind the battlements again and again. She had to .... New York as a result of this incident.

Summary skills 2

Here are some pictures illustrating the San Francisco disaster; but they are not in order. Your task is to find the correct order. Be careful: there is one picture that does not belong to this story.

Guessing unknown words

Match each word in italics in column A with the meaning in column B that
comes closest to it. Column B has some extra meanings.

COLUMN A

1 This catastrophe is due ... entirely to *ill-will* between
   the stage staff and the soprano. (line 2)
2 ... after several *stormy* rehearsals, ... (line 5)
3 ... to complete her first performance without *mishap*
   ... (line 7)
4 ... she *hurls* herself off and lands on a mattress....
   (line 10)
5 ... now laughing in delirious *glee*, ... (line 17)
6 Alas, it is thus that fatal errors are *engendered*.
   (line 33)
7 ... a group of soldiers marched on to the stage but
   stopped *dead in its tracks* ... (line 49)
8 ... she made a series of violently negative *gestures* ...
   (line 55)

COLUMN B

a) pretending to be shot
b) joy
c) in bad weather
d) hand movements
e) marches
f) full of disagreement
g) planned
h) bad planning
i) throws
j) born
k) suddenly and absolutely
l) something going wrong
m) bad feelings

Accurate comprehension

Mark each sentence with **T** if it is true according to the text and **F** if it is false
according to the text.

1 People often go to see more than one opera each year at the City Center in
   New York.
2 In both the performances described Tosca was played by a fat woman.
3 The author of the text is sure that Tosca bounced exactly 15 times in the New
   York performance.
4 *Tosca* is an 'easy' opera for a producer, according to the author of the text.
5 The first-act chorus in *Tosca* sings on stage.
6 The boys in the firing squad liked opera very much.
7 The disaster in San Francisco was the fault of the execution squad.

Unit 16   The poisoning of Michigan

This text is difficult, but if you read it slowly and carefully, twice, and then do the exercises, you will be able to understand it.

IN THE spring of 1973 a truck driver, remembered only as Shorty, made a routine delivery from a chemical factory in Central Michigan to an agricultural feed plant in another part of the State. The plant's workers unloaded a ton of what they believed was magnesium oxide, a crumbly whitish substance, packed in heavy brown paper sacks on which a trade name was crudely stencilled. Over the next few weeks this was mixed into tons of cattle feed and sent to farm suppliers throughout Michigan.

In fact, a hideous mistake had been made. Whoever loaded Shorty's truck filled it not with magnesium oxide, a harmless antacid which was often added to dairy cattle feed to improve milk production, but with almost identical sacks of a similar-looking substance — polybrominated biphenyl (PBB). This was an industrial chemical, developed to bond with hard plastics and make them fireproof, and it was highly toxic.

The two chemicals, produced in different buildings at Michigan Chemical Corporation's factory, should have been kept in separate warehouses, and dispatched from different loading areas. They weren't — and afterwards no one could explain how the mistake was made. Neither Shorty, nor the men who handled the bags at either end of his trip, noticed the difference. Given that magnesium oxide was sold under the trade name of Nutrimaster, and PBB under the name of Firemaster; that some of the lettering on the bags was smudged; that some of the mixer operators were barely literate — the mix-up was understandable. Yet no one had envisaged it, and so tens of thousands of Michigan cattle were poisoned, and the poisoning spread to everyone who consumed Michigan beef and milk.

It was not a single disaster. Cattle ate contaminated feed day after day for months before one farmer, with an exceptional knowledge of chemicals, was able to track down the reason why so many of his animals had sickened and died. Working in isolation he had no idea that other farmers were suffering too— and each of them also assumed that the undiagnosed plague which devastated his herd was unique.

The farmers sent their unprofitable animals, and what milk they produced, to market. Consequently, for at least nine months, heavily contaminated meat and dairy products were widely sold in Michigan supermarkets. When a thorough investigation of the human health effects was eventually made, it was estimated that all of Michigan's nine million inhabitants had ingested enough PBB to accumulate a body burden of a chemical so persistent that traces would remain in their tissues for the rest of their lives.

By then the experts had discovered that PBB can wreak havoc with the liver, the central nervous system, the bones and the immunity system. It crosses the placenta to the foetus, and shows up in the breast milk of nursing moth-

105 ers. It is suspected of causing cancer and genetic damage.

When Michigan was contaminated, the only poisoning of which most local doctors 110 had experience was the acute kind which makes people immediately ill. They failed to understand a chronic toxicosis which builds up over months, slowly retarding bodily functions, and for a 115 long time they insisted that PBB appeared to do no damage.

'We were mired in a swamp of ignorance,' Michigan's 120 Director of Public Health later admitted.

(From an article by Joyce Egginton in *The Observer*.)

cattle: cows are female cattle; bulls are male cattle.   *harmless*: something that is harmless cannot hurt anyone.
barely literate: not able to read or write very well.
that the undiagnosed plague which devastated his herd was unique: that he was the only farmer
   whose cattle were being killed by a sickness he did not understand.
traces: very, very small amounts.   *foetus*: child that has not yet been born, but is still inside its mother.

Summary skills 1 : what next?

Here is a chart of the main events in the article, in the order in which they happened. (Like many articles and stories, this one does not tell the events in the exact order they happened.) Fill in the blank spaces on the chart.

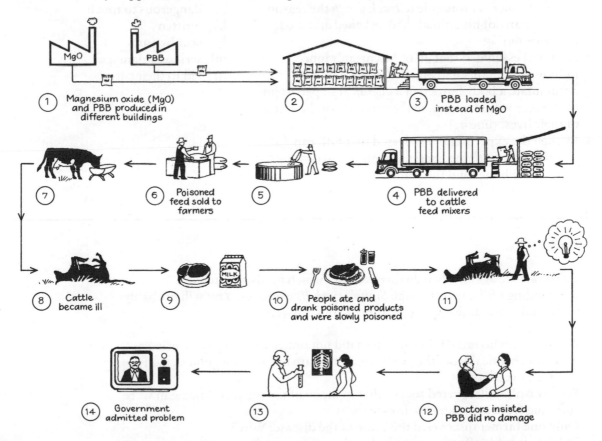

1. Magnesium oxide (MgO) and PBB produced in different buildings
2.
3. PBB loaded instead of MgO
4. PBB delivered to cattle feed mixers
5.
6. Poisoned feed sold to farmers
7.
8. Cattle became ill
9.
10. People ate and drank poisoned products and were slowly poisoned
11.
12. Doctors insisted PBB did no damage
13.
14. Government admitted problem

Summary skills 2

At what five places on the chart did someone do his or her job badly? Do not hesitate to look back at the text.

Guessing unknown words

Match each italicized word in column A with the meaning in column B that comes closest to it. Column B has some extra meanings.

COLUMN A

1 ... packed in heavy brown paper sacks on which a trade name was crudely *stencilled*. (line 14)
2 This was an industrial chemical, developed to *bond* with hard plastics and make them fireproof. (line 31)
3 ... and it was highly *toxic*. (line 33)
4 The two chemicals ... should have been ... *dispatched* from different loading areas. (line 39)
5 ... that some of the lettering on the bags was *smudged*; ... (line 53)
6 ... one farmer ... was able to *track down* the reason why so many of his animals had sickened and died. (lines 68–69)
7 ... it was estimated that all of Michigan's nine million inhabitants had *ingested* enough PBB to accumulate a body burden of a chemical so persistent that traces would remain in their tissues for the rest of their lives. (line 91)
8 By then the experts had discovered that PBB can *wreak havoc with* the liver, the central nervous system, the bones and the immunity system. (lines 98–99)

COLUMN B

a) attach itself to
b) missing
c) eaten
d) explain
e) difficult to read
f) stored
g) compete
h) find
i) poisonous
j) dangerous to touch
k) written
l) sent by truck
m) seriously damage
n) fed to their cattle

Why?

Read the article again. Then do this exercise, which needs a better understanding of the text than the *Summary skills* exercises. You will probably want to look back at the text to be sure of your answers.

1 The people who mixed the cattle feed did not notice that they were using a different chemical from the usual one. There are five reasons; find as many of the five as you can.
2 Why wasn't it discovered sooner that so many of the cattle in Michigan were suffering from a mysterious disease?
3 Only one farmer discovered the cause of the disease. Why?
4 PBB has terrible effects on people, but these were not discovered for a long time. Why?

Negative expressions

Negative expressions do not always contain 'not' or 'no'. For example, in the sentence

> 'She could have told me earlier!'

the words *could have* carry a negative meaning; it is clear that 'she did not tell me earlier'.

You probably know most of the 'negative expressions' in English, but if you read carelessly you can miss them, and misunderstand a sentence completely.

In this exercise, underline or note the negative expressions and write a sentence with 'not' in it for each situation.

1 The plant's workers unloaded a ton of what they believed was magnesium oxide.
2 The two chemicals should have been kept in separate warehouses.
3 Neither Shorty, nor the men who handled the bags at either end of the trip, noticed the difference.
4 They failed to understand a chronic toxicosis which builds up over months.

Part 5   *Persuasion: Why you should do it*

Unit 17   The challenge

The advertisement opposite appeared in a British newspaper. Read it carefully, more than once if you wish, before doing the exercises.

Summary skills

Complete the following table about the two cars. Do not bother to put details: just put a √ for the car that does better in each category. The first two are done for you as an example.

You may want to look back at the text to check your answers.

	Audi 80 GLS	BL Princess
Price		√
Reliability	√	
Comfort: elbow room		
headroom		
legroom (rear)		
Speed: 0–60 mph		
50–70 mph in 3rd gear		
Economy: type of petrol used		
mpg		
money saved over 30,000 miles		

It's surprising what £100 can buy you these days.

Princess 2000HLS £5,791   **Audi 80 GLS £5,887**

Just the other day, we at Audi chanced upon an advertisement for the BL Princess.

Naturally, most of the advertisement was devoted to championing the Princess's many virtues.

Towards the end, however, the makers of the Princess issued a very interesting challenge.

They said, "...we challenge you to find another car in its class which now approaches it for reliability, comfort, performance or economy."

Well, with a price difference of only £96, the Audi 80 GLS is certainly in the same class.

But just how well does it match up?

Not being people to shirk a challenge, we'll take those points one by one.

RELIABILITY
Reliability is very difficult to assess, of course.

However, a recent independent consumer study showed that the Audi 80 GLS was above average for reliability, while the Princess was rated below average.

COMFORT
The Princess has built itself an excellent reputation as a large, comfortable saloon.

Surprisingly, though, the Audi 80 actually has 1" more elbow room on average, and 1½" more headroom. (The Princess, to be fair, does have ½" more legroom in the rear.)

PERFORMANCE
According to Autocar, the Audi 80 GLS is 2½ seconds faster from 0-60 mph, over one second faster from 50-70 mph in third gear, and goes on to a higher top speed.

ECONOMY
Again according to Autocar, the Audi 80 GLS achieves 28.2 mpg overall on 2-star petrol compared with the Princess's 24.1 mpg overall on 4-star petrol.

At current prices, that could amount to a saving of about £240 over 30,000 miles.

THE AUDI CHALLENGE
Our challenge is quite straightforward: drive both. Put the 80 GLS through its paces. Do the same with the Princess 2000 HLS.

You'll be surprised how much difference £100 can make.

The Audi 80 GLS.
Audi The car for now.

(From an advertisement for Audi.)

reliability: a person or thing that is reliable can be trusted.

1": one inch.
assess: judge.

mph: miles per hour.
mpg: miles per gallon.

Guessing unknown words

Use what you find in the text, what you know about similar words, and what you know about the world, to guess the probable meaning of each word.

1 *chanced upon* (line 4): You probably know that *by chance* means *by accident*. So *chanced upon* probably means ....
2 *championing . . . virtues* (line 7): The fact that it was an advertisement tells you that this probably means *saying* ....
3 *challenge* (lines 10, 11): If you *challenge* someone to do something, and that person does it, how do you feel?
4 *match up* (line 16): If something doesn't *match up* to your expectations, it is .... than you expected.
5 *shirk* (line 17): When a person *shirks* his duties you describe him as ....
6 *saloon* (line 27) is a type of ....
7 *straightforward* (line 45) probably means ....
8 *Put the 80 GLS through its paces* (line 46): From line 45, you can guess that this probably means ....

Inference

The authors of this text are trying to communicate several things that they do not say directly. For example, when they write *the Princess's many virtues*, they want you to think, 'The Princess is a good car (so if the Audi is better, it must be very good).'

In this exercise, match each phrase from the text (in column A) with the idea the authors are trying to communicate (in column B). There are some extra answers in column B.

COLUMN A
1 a price difference of only £96 (line 14)
2 an independent consumer study (line 21)
3 to be fair (line 30)
4 at current prices (line 42)
5 our challenge is quite straightforward (line 45)

COLUMN B
a) This may increase with time.
b) The other one was not independent.
c) This is the truth, not just our opinion.
d) The other one asked you to measure things and read studies.
e) This is very modern.
f) This is not much.
g) We are not hiding facts that are to our disadvantage.

Unit 18　Go ahead – read this

"I know what—let's stay in and get some fresh air."

Reading for specific information

Here is a table summarizing the points made in the leaflet on the next page.
Copy the table and fill in the empty spaces by looking back at the text. Do not
worry about writing complete sentences: just make notes that you and your
teacher can understand. If you are not sure of an answer, put a question mark
after it. Perhaps you will want to discuss the answers in small groups.

Problem	Exact cause	Result	If there were no private cars, ...
Air pollution	Carbon monoxide & benzyprene & nitrates		
Space pollution		Crowding?	More homes, gardens, places to work & play
Noise pollution			
Accidents	Text does not say		

Go ahead. Read this. You don't have to watch the road the way you do when you drive the car.

CONGRATULATIONS!

By riding public transportation, you are helping to solve some of the major pollution problems plaguing Boston.   5
1. *AIR POLLUTION.* Motor vehicles powered by internal combustion engines are responsible for over 80 percent of the deadly carbon monoxide as well as the cancer-causing benzpyrene and nitrates in the air. Eighty-nine percent of the vehicles on the road in Massachusetts are privately owned   10
   and are often operated with only one person in the car. If people would use public transportation instead of their cars, air pollution levels could be significantly lowered.
2. *SPACE POLLUTION.* Thirty percent of the land in downtown Boston is devoted to cars. Where there are garages, there   15
   could be gardens. Where there are highways, there should be homes and places to work and play.
3. *NOISE POLLUTION.* Studies show that people today show a greater hearing loss with age than ever before. Much of this is due to honking horns, loud engines and general traffic   20
   noise.

The cost of a personal car is high to the individual. The average person pays about $2000 per car per year in depreciation, gasoline, insurance, taxes, and maintenance. *But for society as a whole, personal cars are a luxury we cannot*   25
afford. We pay in death from auto accidents, in poor health from air pollution, in loss of hearing from noise pollution, and in the destruction of our cities by the ever increasing number of highways.

HOW YOU CAN HELP: 30
1. DO NOT DRIVE IN THE CITY.
2. Walk, whenever possible, or ride a bike.
3. Use public transportation.
4. Oppose legislation calling for more highways in the cities.
5. *Support legislation for improving public transportation*   35
   facilities.

For further information, contact Boston Area Ecology Action, 925 Mass. Ave., Cambridge, 876-7085. Please pass this on to a friend.

(From *The Environmental Handbook.*)

Guessing unknown words

Here is a list of words and expressions from the text. Some of them are words you have not seen before; you may know some of them; and some of them may be familiar words used in a new way. Choose an appropriate word for each blank in the sentences below the list. (You will not use all the words.)

a) plaguing (line 5)
b) vehicle (lines 6, 10)
c) significantly (line 13)
d) devoted to (line 15)
e) due to (line 20)
f) honking (line 20)
g) ever (line 28)
h) calling for (line 34)
i) facilities (line 36)
j) privately (line 10)

1 Fires in the home are often .... carelessness.
2 Our local newspaper has one page .... news about minority groups – blacks, Asians, and Indians living in Britain and especially in our area.
3 The town of Wantage has excellent recreational ....: a swimming pool, three tennis courts, two squash courts, a gymnasium and several playing fields.
4 Studies have shown that babies fed on mothers' milk are .... healthier than bottle-fed babies.
5 As more people live longer, national budgets will have to change to provide for the .... growing percentage of the population over 65.
6 I was driving behind an enormous truck yesterday, with a sign on the back saying 'Long ....'.
7 The Centre for Handicapped Children is run by the state now, but at the beginning it was .... financed.
8 I would have slept all morning if a car .... outside my window hadn't woken me up.

Accurate comprehension

Mark **T** for the sentences that are true according to the text and **F** for the sentences that are false according to the text. You will probably want to look back at the text to check your answers.

1 Cars driven with only one person in each car are responsible for 80% of air pollution.
2 In Boston, 30% of the land is taken up by highways, streets and garages.
3 Loud noises can make people lose their hearing.
4 Pollution by cars costs $2,000 per person per year.
5 Better public transportation is a very effective way of lowering the pollution level in Boston.

Unit 19   Save the children

Here is an advertisement from an American women's magazine. Read it twice, taking as much time as you want.

Save The Children Federation® 48 Wilton Road, Westport, Connecticut 06880

PLEASE READ MY URGENT PLEA
TO HELP SAVE MARIA PASTORA
AND THE OTHER CHILDREN OF HER VILLAGE

Dear Ms. Reader:

    Imagine an 11-year old child whose days are often spent scrubbing clothes, raising a baby 　　5
brother, struggling with heavy farm chores.
    Imagine a little girl who knows there will not be enough food for dinner. Who can't fill
her stomach with water because it's contaminated. Who has watched life slip away from her
father and her little brother and sister because the family could not afford a doctor.
    Hard to believe? For Maria Pastora, these are the facts of life. 　　10
    Maria would gladly walk miles to school, but her mother, now alone, needs her badly at
home. Chances are Maria will grow up illiterate. Her future? In many ways, disastrous.
    But for just 52 pennies a day, you can sponsor a child like Maria. Show her that somewhere,
someone cares about her plight. Through Save the Children, you can help Maria's mother get
the tools and guidance she needs to turn their meager half-acre into a source of good food; 　　15
earn the money she needs to buy clothing and school supplies for Maria.
    To help Maria most, your money is combined with that of other sponsors, so hardworking
people can help themselves. Build a school...a health facility...reclaim land...bring in
clean water. This is what Save the Children has been about since 1932.
    For you there are many rewards. The chance to correspond with your sponsored child. 　　20
Receive photographs, progress reports. Know you are reaching out to another human being. Not
with a handout, but a hand up. That's how Save the Children works. But without you, it can't
work. Please take a moment now to fill out and mail the coupon below to help a child like
Maria and her village.
    It can make such a difference...in her life and yours. 　　25

For the childen,

David L. Guyer
Executive Director

(from an advertisement for the Save the Children Federation.)

Not with a handout, but a hand up: not just by giving money, but by helping people to become independent.

Summary skills

Choose one subject from the following list and read the text again, making notes about the subject you have chosen. Your notes do not have to be in complete sentences.

When you have finished the notes, find one or two other people in the class who have chosen the same subject as you. Compare your notes and write a new set of notes that you agree on.

Subjects:
1 School.
2 Maria's mother.
3 Food and water.
4 Sponsoring a child.
5 Maria's family life.

Guessing unknown words

Match each word in italics in column A with the meaning in column B that comes closest to it. Column B has some extra meanings.

COLUMN A
1 Imagine an 11-year-old child whose days are often spent *scrubbing* clothes, ... (line 5)
2 ... raising a baby brother, *struggling with* heavy farm chores. (line 6)
3 ... raising a baby brother, struggling with heavy farm *chores*. (line 6)
4 Who can't fill her stomach with water because it's *contaminated*. (line 8)
5 Chances are Maria will grow up *illiterate*. (line 12)
6 Show her that somewhere, someone cares about her *plight*. (line 14)
7 ... you can help Maria's mother get the tools and guidance she needs to turn their *meager* half-acre into a source of good food; ... (line 15)
8 To help Maria most, your money is combined with that of other *sponsors*, ... (line 17)

COLUMN B
a) serious problem
b) in bad health
c) washing
d) jobs
e) buying
f) having great difficulty with
g) small
h) machines
i) people who provide money
j) dirty
k) organizations
l) not able to read or write

Find the reasons ... find the ways

This exercise will give you practice in finding connections between different parts of a text. Answer each question in a few words; do not bother to write complete sentences.

1 Find three reasons why Maria is in danger of falling ill.
2 Find the reason Maria's mother is alone.
3 Find three things that could help Maria go to school.
4 Find two things that could keep Maria healthier.
5 Find three ways in which a sponsor communicates with a child.

Unit 20   Two letters

These letters were received by a man who owed money to an American doctor.
The doctor had treated the man's wife.

G. R. BROWN M.D.
4231 ████████, ████████, Texas 77002

November 5, 1981

Mr George ███████████
3124 ████████████████
███████, Texas 77005

Re: $325.00
    Marion ████████████
    Account No. ████

Dear Mr ████████████

    Two weeks ago we wrote to you asking you to contact us
about the above account; as yet we have not heard from you.
    At the time Mrs ████████ needed medical attention she
was treated immediately. We feel that you should at least
extend the courtesy of replying to our several requests
for payment by making full or partial payments, beginning
now. Even small payments will be accepted if they are
regular ones.
    We expect to hear from you within the next
two weeks, please.

Very truly yours,

Helen Marques

Helen Marques
Office Manager

G. R. BROWN M.D.
4231 ████████, ████████, Texas 77002

November 17, 1981

Mr George ███████████
3124 ████████ ████
███████, Texas 77005

Re: $325.00
    Marion ████████████
    Account No. ████

Dear Mr ████████████

    We cannot understand why you continue to ignore the requests
for payment we have been mailing to you. We feel that you
have had ample time to send payment, call, or write regarding
this account.
    If we have not heard from you within two weeks, we shall
have no alternative than to turn this account over to a
collection agency for payment. Surely you do not want
to have this on your credit record.
    We expect prompt attention to this matter.

Very truly yours,

Helen Marques

Helen Marques
Office Manager

M.D.: Medical Doctor.

Have you got the main ideas?

Perhaps you can do this exercise without looking back at the letters. If not, the questions will help you to find the main ideas. Mark **T** if the sentence is true according to the letters, and **F** if it is false according to the letters.

1 The 5 November letter was the first one from Dr Brown's office about the money the man owed.
2 The 5 November letter is more polite than the 17 November letter.
3 Helen Marques thinks that $325.00 is a small payment.
4 The 17 November letter contains a threat.
5 In two weeks Ms Marques will write the same man another letter.

Guessing unknown words

Find words or phrases in the two letters which have roughly the meanings given below.

1 Record of a patient's bills.
2 Be polite, and answer.
3 Pay no attention to.
4 Enough.
5 Other choice.
6 Company that specializes in getting money from people who owe it.

Inference

Find evidence in the two letters for the following:
1 Several people work for Dr Brown.
2 Studies have shown that most people prefer to pay large debts in several payments.
3 If the man telephoned the doctor's office and explained that he was on strike and had no money, they would probably be understanding.
4 Information about the way people pay their debts is centralized in the United States.

Part 6   Categories: How things are classified

Unit 21   Elephants

Here is a text from a book about plants and animals. Read it once, slowly; then read it again if you wish.

Millions of years ago the elephant order was very large; there were many types, both large and small, and even some with four tusks. As late as the Stone age, great woolly mammoths with immense curved tusks roamed Europe, Asia and North America. Today the order is reduced to only two species, the African and Indian elephants.   5

African elephants have bigger ears and tusks than the smaller Indian elephants; they also have a flatter forehead and a concave back. Their tusks develop from incisor teeth in the upper jaw which grow up to 3·5 metres long in males but are much smaller in females. So many African elephants have been hunted for their valuable ivory   10
tusks that the species is now quite rare and most of the survivors are in game reserves. The Indian elephant has been domesticated for centuries to carry large loads and perform other heavy work. Only the male Indian elephants bear tusks, and these are used for defence, to uproot trees and to dig for roots and water.   15

Elephants are the largest of all land animals. The African bush elephant is the greatest in size, with males growing up to 3·5 metres tall and weighing up to six tons. Elephants have just one enormous

ridged molar (cheek tooth) in each half of each jaw, which is used for
crushing food. When a molar wears out it is replaced by another one   20
from behind it. An elephant is mature at 15 years and usually dies at
the age of 60. Cow elephants produce one offspring every two years.
The young calf takes 21 months to develop inside the mother and then
takes five years to be fully weaned. The gestation period is the longest
of all mammals in comparison with nine months in man and three   25
weeks or less in mice.

The elephant's trunk is an elongated nose (proboscis). It is prehen-
sile (gripping) and is used for gathering food, often up to 100 kg per
day of leaves, tree bark, grass and roots. Its delicate tip, which has
one finger-like projection in the Indian, and two in the African   30
elephant, can pick up small objects. The elephant drinks by sucking
up water with its trunk which is then squirted into its mouth. It can
give itself a shower-bath of water or mud in the same way. Although
elephants have poor sight they have a keen sense of smell. When they
move their trunks from side to side or raise them in the air they are   35
smelling out their surroundings.

(From *The Penguin book of the natural world.*)

concave: curved inward (see the picture on page 84).
ivory: Ivory is creamy white. It is used to make jewellery and to cover the white keys on a piano.
weaned: A baby that is fully weaned drinks no more milk from its mother.

Summary skills 1

Choose one subject from the following list and read the text again, making brief
notes about the subject you have chosen. It is not necessary to write complete
sentences.

When you have finished your notes, find one or two other people in the class
who have chosen the same subject as you. Compare your notes and write new
notes that you agree on.

Subjects:
1 The African elephant.
2 The Indian elephant.
3 Teeth, tusks and trunks.
4 A female elephant's life.

Summary skills 2

Here are pictures of an African elephant and an Indian elephant. Describe in a
few words the difference indicated by each letter. 1a and 2a are done for you as
examples.

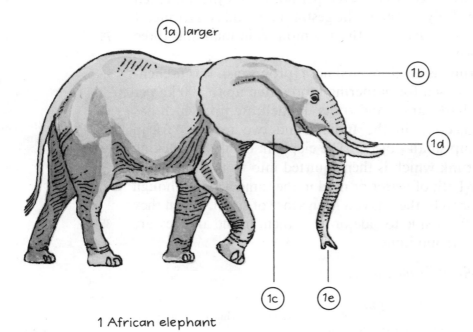

1 African elephant

2 Indian elephant

Guessing unknown words

Match each word or phrase in italics in column A with the meaning in column B
that comes closest to it. Column B has some extra meanings.

COLUMN A

1 Elephants have just one enormous ridged molar
   (cheek tooth) in each half of each *jaw*, which is used
   for crushing food. (line 19)
2 The Indian elephant *has been domesticated* for
   centuries to carry large loads and perform other
   heavy work. (line 12)
3 Cow elephants produce one *offspring* every two
   years. (line 22)
4 The *gestation period* is the longest of all mammals in
   comparison with nine months in man and three
   weeks or less in mice. (line 24)
5 The elephant's trunk is an *elongated* nose
   (proboscis). (line 27)
6 Its delicate *tip*, which has one finger-like projection in
   the Indian, ... (line 29)
7 The elephant drinks by sucking up water with its
   trunk which is then *squirted* into its mouth. (line 32)
8 ... they have a *keen* sense of smell. (line 34)

COLUMN B

a) bad
b) pointed end
c) has been tamed
d) time it takes to get first teeth
e) blown
f) the bone where teeth grow
g) what elephants use to crush
   food
h) sharp
i) colour
j) young elephant
k) time a baby takes to develop
   inside the mother
l) sucked
m) new tooth
n) has had its tusks removed
o) longer than usual

Accurate comprehension

For each sentence, mark **T** if it is true according to the text, **F** if it is false
according to the text, and **DS** if the text doesn't say.

1 In classifying animals, *species* is a smaller category than *order*.
2 African elephants' jaws can grow up to 3·5 metres in length.
3 There are more African elephants than Indian elephants.
4 An elephant has four teeth in its mouth.
5 Some elephants can pick up 100 kg weights with their trunks.
6 Cow elephants sometimes have three calves drinking their milk.

Unit 22 Airports

Here is an article from a financial newspaper. It was written in the month of June. Read it carefully, twice, before you do the exercises.

MOVES BY the British Airports Authority to persuade more passengers to use Gatwick are having an impact on Heathrow.

5

Heathrow is still the largest airport in Britain and one of the largest in the world with its capacity of 30m passengers a year. But latest figures from the

10 authority show that passenger traffic last month at Gatwick grew four times faster than Heathrow compared with the same month last year.

15

More than 2.2m passengers used Heathrow last month, 7 per cent up on the previous May. In comparison, 687,700 passengers used Gatwick, a rise of 26 per

20 cent on the same month last year.

Stansted, Essex, improved its growth record last month, at 13.9 per cent. It is double that of

25 Heathrow.

The marked growth at Gatwick was mainly because of the move of all whole-charter flights after April 1 from Heathrow and

30 Stansted. This was designed to take the pressure off Heathrow

and use the new capacity at Gatwick, where a £100m, six-year expansion programme has been completed.

35

This has boosted capacity to 16m passengers a year, but in the year to the end of May only 6.8m passengers used the airport. The authority wanted to use this

40 spare capacity by boosting the number of scheduled flights to and from Gatwick. These moves, backed by the Government, have failed.

45

Persuasion

The authority is concentrating on persuading airlines serving Canada, Spain and Portugal to use Gatwick as their UK base.

50

The Government has used the bilateral route talks with Canada to raise the issue of Air Canada's withdrawing from Heathrow for Gatwick.

55

The authority said last night that success would mean the reciprocal transfer of all British Airways flights between the UK and Canada to Gatwick.

60

(From an article by Lynton McLain in *The Financial Times*.)

30m: 30 million   *whole-charter flights*: Unlike regular flights, whole-charter flights only operate on certain specific dates. Tickets for these flights are cheaper and cannot be exchanged

---

Summary skills 1

Fill in this table as completely as you can. You will have to leave some spaces blank.

	Gatwick	Heathrow	Stansted
Capacity			
Passengers in May			
% rises in passengers since May last year			
Passengers this year to the end of May			

Summary skills 2

1 Name one category of flights that leaves from Gatwick.
2 Where do flights to Canada leave from, according to the article?

Guessing unknown words

Find *single* words in the text which seem to correspond to the meanings given below.

Example (lines 1–10): effect
Answer: impact (line 4)

1 (lines 22 to 35) very noticeable
2 (lines 36 to 45) increased
3 (lines 36 to 45) regular

4 (lines 51 to 60) question to discuss
5 (lines 51 to 60) similar, but in the opposite direction

Making connections

Misunderstandings sometimes happen because we do not realize which person or thing is meant by a word like *she* or *this*. This exercise will give you practice in making connections between words like these and their meanings. Give the meaning of each word or phrase in italics. (The meaning can be in the same sentence or elsewhere in the text.)

1 Heathrow is still the largest airport in Britain and one of the largest in the world with *its* capacity of 30m passengers a year. (line 7)
2 ... a rise of 26 per cent on *the same month* last year. (line 20)
3 *It* is double *that* of Heathrow. (line 24)
4 *This* was designed to take the pressure off Heathrow ... (line 30)
5 *This* has boosted capacity to 16m passengers a year, ... (line 36)
6 ... but in the year to the end of May only 6·8m passengers used *the airport*. (line 39)
7 *These moves*, backed by the government, have failed. (line 43)

Accurate comprehension

For each sentence, mark **T** if it is true according to the text, **F** if it is false according to the text, and **DS** if the text doesn't say.

1 Stansted traffic has grown twice as fast as Heathrow traffic since last May.
2 Other categories of flights besides whole-charter flights have been moved to Gatwick since April 1.
3 Expansion at Gatwick was begun about six years ago.
4 Gatwick has been less than half-full, on average, since the beginning of the year.
5 Canada will only transfer her flights to Gatwick if Britain transfers hers first.

Unit 23　The trials of an O in a world of Xs

Most people have had the experience of being alone in a group of people very different from themselves: being much older or much younger than everybody else, being of the opposite sex or a different race from everyone else, being a city person in the country or a country person in the city.

Here is an American text about being different in the place where you work. The characters are called Xs and Os. These terms are from a game where the opposing markers are Xs and Os; so an X could be considered as the opposite of an O.

Read the whole text carefully before beginning the exercises. Read it twice if you like.

1

The O's uniqueness gets it **X**-tra attention. We're distracted by the O; the O gets stared at – it's a novelty. People will remember more about the O than about any of the **X**'s.

2

There will be more gossip about the O, more stories and rumours about the O: *"Did you hear what happened in Dallas?" "I heard they gave that sales job to an O." "No kidding! What's gonna happen next?" "I don't know, but I sure hope I don't have to work for one."*

3

The O is always performing in the spotlight and subject to public scrutiny. The O cannot hide its mistakes as easily as the **X**'s can. And people make sure the O knows it.

"You are our test O, and we're watching you. If you do well, we might get more O's."

"We've never had anyone like you before, and we're dying to know how it will work out."

4

This scrutiny can make the O feel that it's walking a tightrope. Even the smallest mistake could be fatal. Sometimes the X's envy the O's for the special attention and publicity they get. But the O's great visibility is not the kind that brings power and advancement, because what we're noticing is not the O's competence . . .

5

but its O-ness – whatever it is makes the O different. Sometimes people don't hear a word the O says. They're too busy just staring at it. (That's why O-ness is a burden).

6

Thus O's often have to live up to two (sometimes conflicting) standards: first, whether they can demonstrate the same **X**-pertise as the **X**'s, and . . .

7

second, how well they live up to the **X**'s idea of a "good O."

8

Being the Only or representative O also gives the O an **X**-tra job to do: serving as spokesO – talking for all O's. The O might be sent off to public events as a show O. Or turned to in meetings and asked, "What do you O's think?" The O will be asked to join committees, or to speak "at our next program – devoted entirely to the problems of O's."

9

For the O, this often results in O-verload. (And then the X's wonder why "O's can't take the heat.")

Line numbers in margin: 5, 10, 15, 20, 25 (left column); 30, 35, 40, 45, 50 (right column)

---

performing in the spotlight: like an actress in a dark theatre with a strong light on her: people watch everything she does.
competence: ability to do its job.
burden: heavy weight to carry.
X-pertise: (=expertise) expert ability to do something.
conflicting standards: different ideas of how things should be.

Summary skills

Match each of the numbered sections of the text to one of the illustrations.
There are some illustrations on the next page.

a

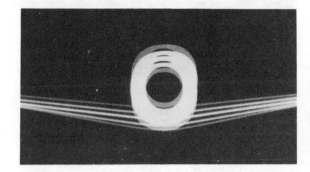

b

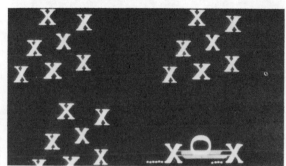

c

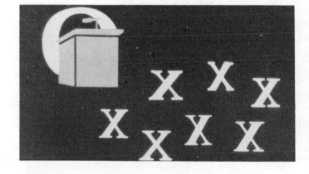

d

e

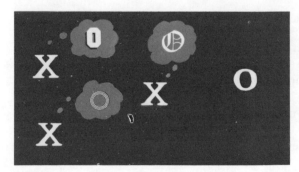

f

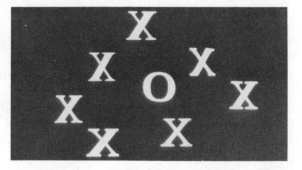

89

g

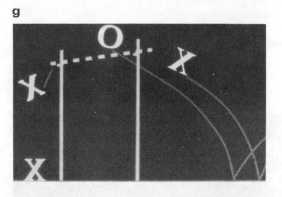

h

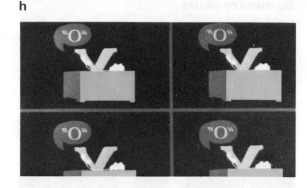

i

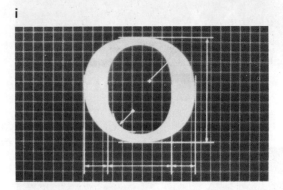

(From *A tale of 'O': On being different
in organizations,* by Rosabeth Moss Kanter
with Barry A. Stein.)

Guessing unknown words

Here is a list of words from the text. Some of them are words you have not seen
before, but you may know some of them. Choose an appropriate word for each
blank in the sentences below the list. (You will not use all the words.)

a) uniqueness (line 1)   e) visibility (line 26)
b) novelty (line 3)   f) spokesperson (*spokesO*, line 42)
c) gossip (line 6)   g) overload (line 49)
d) scrutiny (line 14)

1 The Basque language is not related to any other language in the world. This
  .... has puzzled linguists for years.
2 I was acting as a .... for the other employees, so I was careful not to
  express my personal views.
3 Whenever I go to the village shop, I hear good-natured .... about
  my next-door neighbour and her inventions.
4 Careful .... of the victim's wounds revealed that a heavy object had
  been used.
5 There are not enough telephone lines in our sector, so an .... can
  easily happen.

General to particular

The text describes several different situations, in a general way. The following short passages give particular examples of some of these situations. Find which ones.

a) 'I'm the only black man in my office, and sometimes I take important work home to do. In the office I feel that everybody's always looking at me and it makes me nervous.'
b) A man robbed a bank. He was not wearing a mask but he had covered all his teeth with aluminium foil. Nobody remembered anything about his appearance but his teeth.
c) 'She's a good accounts executive, but she's inhuman – not married, no kids, . . .'
d) 'How do you expect us men to work properly with that female bricklayer on the job?'
e) The President of the United States entered a ten-mile footrace and had to stop after six miles. The story was in all the papers.

"I'm sorry, Billington, you just don't seem to fit."

Unit 24   Wonder wander

Here is a poem by an American author. Read it slowly, as many times as you
like, before doing the exercises.

---

in the afternoon the children walk like ducks
like geese
like from here to there
eyeing bird-trees puppy dogs candy windows
sun balls ice cream wagons   5
lady bugs rose bushes fenced yards vacant lots
tall buildings
and other things
big business men take big business walks
wear big business clothes   10
carry big business briefcases   talk about
big business affairs in
big business voices
young girls walk pretty on the streets
stroll the avenues linger by   15
shop windows   wedding rings   lady hats
shiny dresses   fancy shoes
whisper like turkey hens   passing the time
young men stride on parade   dream headed
wild eyed   eating up the world   20
with deep glances   rubbing empty fingers
in the empty pockets and
planning
me, I wander around soft-shoed   easy-legged
watching the scene as it goes   25
finding things   sea-gull feathers   pink baby roses
everytime I see a letter on the sidewalk
I stop and look   it might be
for me

(By Lenore Kandel, in *I took my mind a walk*.)

Summary skills 1

This poem has five parts. On which line does each part begin?

Summary skills 2

Look back at the text to complete this table. Just put a $\sqrt{}$ in the appropriate box. 'Business men' is done for you as an example.

	children	business men	young girls	young men	me
thinking of future					
thinking of present					
walking without definite direction					
walking without stopping		$\sqrt{}$			
have a plan		$\sqrt{}$			
have no plan					
looking at things					
not looking at things		$\sqrt{}$			

Guessing unknown words

Use the text to guess the probable meaning of each word.

1 *briefcases* (line 11): They are probably made of .... and probably contain ....
2 *linger* (line 15): If young girls do it by shop windows to see wedding rings, lacy hats, etc., it probably means ....
3 *turkey* (line 18): The word *hens* tells you that this is a kind of ....
4 *sea-gull* (line 26): *Feathers* tells you that this is probably a ....

Families of words

Find as many words as you can that have to do with:

1 walking
2 talking
3 animals
4 clothing
5 seeing

Attitudes and feelings 1

1 Which group of people do you think the narrator ('me') has the least sympathy for?
2 Which group of people do you think the narrator has the most sympathy for?

Attitudes and feelings 2

Here is a list of descriptions. Choose the most appropriate description for each person or group of people in the poem. There are some extra descriptions.

a) Wishing dreamily
b) Looking and hoping
c) Disappointed
d) Worried
e) Open to everything
f) Ambitious
g) Slowly becoming angry
h) Busy